THE NICE GIRL'S GUIDE TO

Talking
Dirty

THE NICE GIRL'S GUIDE TO
Talking Dirty

IGNITE YOUR SEX LIFE WITH NAUGHTY WHISPERS, HOT FANTASIES AND SCREAMS OF PASSION

DR. RUTH NEUSTIFTER

Amorata Press

Published by: AMORATA PRESS,
an imprint of Ulysses Press
P.O. Box 3440
Berkeley, CA 94703
www.amoratapress.com

ISBN13: 978-1-56975-938-7
Library of Congress Control Number: 2011904238

Printed in the United States by Bang Printing

10 9 8 7 6 5 4 3 2

Acquisitions Editor: Kelly Reed
Managing Editor: Claire Chun
Editor: Paula Dragosh
Proofreader: Lauren Harrison
Cover design: Wade Nights
Cover illustration: © crixtina/shutterstock.com
Production: Judith Metzener, Abigail Reser
Dialogue contributor: Cameryn Moore (www.camerynmoore.com)

Distributed by Publishers Group West

This book is dedicated to all women who dare to explore pleasure and the partners who love them for it.

Table of Contents

ONE

An Invitation to Aural Exploration

Cameryn: Hi, Eric, it's Cameryn.

Eric: Hi, Cameryn.

Cameryn: How are you doing tonight?

Eric: Pretty good.

Cameryn: Yeah? I bet we can turn that into really, really great before we finish. What do you think?

Eric: I hope so.

Sexuality is the most intimate form of body language we can experience with our partners and ourselves. But when we combine the physically erotic with verbal enticements, we're able to touch our lovers on a new level. A wanton text message or whisper can arouse memories and anticipation far beyond normal conversation, all the while building a deep romantic bond.

Dirty talk opens the door to sweeter seduction, more passionate lovemaking, and the opportunity to explore how emotionally intimate your relationships can become. Whether you consider yourself an expert in these oral skills or you're just beginning to explore the possibilities, this book will help you discover the pleasure of your own style of seductive linguistics while learning more about your sweetheart's sexuality and your own. Nice girls like you and I can turn out to be the best dirty talkers, and I'm going to show you exactly how you can feel good about talking dirty!

For most of us, this is a radical new way to think about dirty talk. Few of us consider explicit language to be artistic, intimate, or even enticing. It's a foray that we imagine is better left to the young, indelicate, or downright crude. Certainly it's no pursuit for nice girls like us! What would people think if they knew that our lips could utter such inappropriately brazen thoughts in a passionate moment, hours after addressing a lecture hall or a client? Or perhaps there's a deeper reason why dirty talk is taboo.

Indeed, some of the most powerful and verbally skilled women have been celebrated for their ability to tantalize a lucky listener. According to Betsy Prioleua, author of *Seductress: Women Who Ravished the World and Their Lost Art of Love*, "If you study the great seductresses, one thing they had in common was great verbal skills. It was their chief aphrodisiac." In fact, according to Prioleua, some of the greatest seductresses throughout history were not traditionally attractive women. Some didn't even wear makeup or dress up for their lovers! Instead, they were known for their wit and words, which drew men to them like moths to a flame. Could it be that there's a special power in dirty talk, a secret we're not supposed to discover?

Scheherazade, the legendary Persian queen and storyteller, not only saved her own life but seduced her king into fathering children with her and marrying her through the art of sharing one story after another, night after night. No doubt some of these tales were of romance and carnal desire. Now, I'm not suggesting that you memorize one thousand naughty stories. But if Scheherazade could introduce herself to a king and become his queen with nothing but her voice and imagination, perhaps you can offer a few wanton words sure to put a tremble in your sweetheart's knees.

Gaining Confidence

Confidence is an amazing thing. Not only is it deliciously contagious and easy to grow once planted, it also has that handy "fake it till you make it" quality. You've taken an important step toward increasing your own sensual self-assurance simply by joining me for this book. One of the best ways to gain this kind of confidence is to surround yourself with others who have it and believe that you have it, too, even if it's a bit hidden.

How do I know this about you? First of all, I know that it matters to you, because you're holding this book, and that's the most essential ingredient. Second, I've helped many nice girls just like you discover that they really are secretly erotically daring. In fact, I consider you a secret erotic superhero, as you'll see later.

As a sexuality educator, I've worked with many clients who spent months tongue-tied, too shy to tell me why they had even hired me in the first place! Some of them were single when we began to work together; others had long-term partners. Quite a few even brought their sweethearts to our sessions, many of whom were just as shy and benefited just as much.

Nice girls have often learned to keep some of our confidence under wraps, and sometimes we forget about it. Don't worry, I know it's there even if you've lost track of it and need a few reminders of how to get to it. While you're getting back in touch with that inner strength, you'll learn how to fake it in fun ways until those sweet somethings slip through your lips as easily as "please" and "thank you." In fact, you might find yourself using more of those words in naughty ways, too.

Best of all, learning to be a savvy dirty talker is fun! Sure, it might raise your anxiety a bit in the beginning, but you'll be glad you pushed yourself as you start to look forward to your next opportunity to drop a subtle hint or unleash a torrid request. One of my favorite clients, Rose, told me about her experience after one of my workshops. She had participated in a couple of the exercises included in this book and found herself feeling inspired. After the workshop ended she joined the hosts, me, and a few other attendees for a late-night bite and a glass of wine at a nearby tapas restaurant.

Rose was boisterous, with a hearty laugh, as we discussed different parts of the workshop and how they applied to our own lives. Still, I remember that she was more eager to ask about others' experiences than to disclose her own. What I didn't know is that she was working up her courage to try dirty talk for the first time with her husband.

After the sangria had her more relaxed, she slipped off to the restroom and quickly typed out a text message for him: "I've had a few glasses of sangria, and it has me wanting you. Don't go to bed before I get home." She sent the message before she had a chance to think twice, knowing he was on the train home and unlikely to have reception. He wouldn't be able to answer right away. Rose then rejoined our group with a blush on her cheeks that didn't come from the wine. Of course, we all noticed, and with a burst of confidence she passed around her phone so we could read what she wrote. Rose's message may sound tame, but it got her intent through very clearly and was sure to get her husband's attention and have him eager for her return!

After her nerves calmed a bit, and with some encouragement from the group, she pulled out her phone again and sent a second message: "I can't stop thinking about you and the way your lips feel on my mouth and . . ." Cheers and whistles erupted from our group as she passed around her phone again. Rose soon decided she had time for a third message before she left to take her train home: "Remember how we used to kiss in high school? If not, I'm ready to remind you. And more." She tucked her phone into her purse, paid her tab, and rushed to catch a train so she could change before her husband arrived home.

Later, Rose dropped me an e-mail to let me know that her husband was too stunned to respond when he got the messages. But he did hop in a cab to rush home, instead of transferring from his train to a slower bus. They're getting better and better at these naughty messages, and Rose is thinking of reading some of them aloud to him soon. Although she was nervous at first, she discovered that it was not only sexy but fun to flirt and tease in this new way.

An Art and a Skill

Now, when I tell you dirty talk is a learned skill, this is not to suggest that I'm on a mission to make you the most crass sailor on the boardwalk! Indeed, the shy blushes and giggles that come with a wanton turn of phrase are a big part of the fun. This is another powerful element of dirty talk: It's taboo, and deep down even nice girls love to be a little bit naughty. This is exactly why I believe that nice girls can be the very best dirty talkers—nobody expects it of us!

That means that when you share a fantasy in midkiss, you're certain to have your lover's immediate attention. The next time you flutter your lashes while offering a particularly intriguing invitation, they'll take special interest, and you'll be racing through their mind until they see you again. And knowing that is sure to rev your own imagination until then, too.

Nice girls are often the best at weaving previously censored thoughts into the most delightful forms of seduction, once we've had a bit of practice and built up our confidence. Furthermore, we're experts at ensuring that the people around us are taken care of and happy. Nice girls are often the first to change their plans to take care of this last-minute crisis or that unexpected problem. We love to see the people around us smile, and many of us live for those rare but wonderful words of thanks.

As an expert on intuiting and leaping to the needs of others, you have the rare ability to bring an integral set of skills to your oral seductions: the element of relational and personal enhancement. By combining a lusty vocabulary with your own personal style of dirty talk, you can guide your relationship to deeper emotional intimacy, right along with the physical. That's right, just like the legendary Scheherazade, you can use the racier side of your imagination to build a strong relationship. Even better, when you seduce your lover, you can also seduce yourself at the very same time.

Aural exploration can be a wonderful way to capture the hearts and loins of your partners, and it can also be a delightful way into your own panties. Learning to find and express your desires has a seductive power all its own. The first time you use this book to devise a tempting script, you may feel more nervous than anything else, but soon you'll discover how fun it is! It won't be long before privately concocting your next flirtation becomes one of your favorite sexy games, no other players needed. Hearing your own voice speak your deepest desires, your hottest fantasies, and your wildest carnal needs is an incredibly hot experience!

I challenge you to be completely honest with yourself as you move through the ideas and activities in this book. This is not a guide on how to please your partner more fully. It's your invitation to increase pleasure in your life and your relationship by finding and unleashing your own inner vixen. As a result, both you and your lover will be curling your toes in excitement! By nurturing and being true to your own sensual self, you're signing up for a more intense experience with this book, in your private life, and in your relationships. It's completely worth the investment, even if you're unsure exactly what turns you on, or you know of only a few things.

Maria and Sam, an adorable young couple, made a habit of skipping seduction and foreplay in favor of diving straight into intercourse. It was fun in the beginning, but by the time they saw me, they were both feeling performance anxiety and a lack of interest in doing anything more than thinking (or complaining) about sex. Maria shared that she was also wondering if there might be a better way to orgasm, but wasn't sure how to initiate that kind of change. Sam had found himself thinking about the possibility of other partners, even though he was dedicated to their monogamous relationship. They knew they needed to change things, but they had never learned how to explore together, or maybe they just forgot how.

Kim and Lisa were both intellectual flirts, with trouble translating their humorous and nerdy banter into something sexy. Instead, they repeated their sexual patterns a few times each month, with neither feeling terribly excited about their sex life.

Shawna came in by herself, and I never did meet her partner. Her goal was to stop withdrawing from sex by figuring out what turned her on and then learning how to ask for it. When I asked Shawna about how sex usually started in her bedroom, she said, "I just lay back and let them do it. That's just how sex works for me and that's what they're used to with all women." But Shawna wanted more, and she was tired of waiting for someone to read her mind.

Sex tends to be very in-the-moment for many couples, as they strive to either concentrate on what's happening right then or on keeping their minds blank. Perhaps they have a few fantasies they enjoy thinking about but are far too shy to discuss without a lot of patience and gentle encouragement in my office. Their lovers may have no idea at all about their secret fantasies! In any case, they're working far too hard to try to make their sexual life just barely good enough when a few important changes could transform it into a naturally erotic experience.

We'll explore how to reveal, nurture, and expand on these hot buttons later. For now, I want you to know that this exploration is not only possible but also can be a sexy activity to do on your own or with a trusted sweetheart. Maria, Sam, Kim, Lisa, and Shawna all found their secret keys to arousal, lighting a sexual spark that turned into a roaring blaze fed by sexy whispers, moans, directions, invitations, and more. Just imagine the fun you'll have discovering your verbal hot spots together and then making the most of them, once you realize how good you are at it!

Key Points

- Dirty talk has a long and creative history! Forget your stereotypes and be ready to immerse yourself in an oral tradition of hot narratives that women have woven for their partners for millennia.
- Aural seduction is a powerful avenue for sexual change in relationships. It makes it possible for us to recognize and communicate our needs at the same time that we seduce our partners.
- For sexy talk to work for you, as well as your partner, it must be an authentic expression of your own desires and turn-ons.

EXERCISE

What is it that you'd like to improve about your love life? How are you hoping dirty talk will help or enhance your own sexuality as well as your relationships? Take a moment to write down these goals. You won't be able to meet your goals until you're sure of what they are, so spend some time considering and refining them.

TWO

Make Time and Space for Pleasure

Cameryn: Well, I'll do my best. I don't think we've spoken before. Do you want to hear a little about me, or do you want to tell me about yourself first?

Eric: Tell me about you.

Cameryn: Okay. Well, I'm forty-four years old. I'm a tall girl, five feet nine inches. I've got [size] forty-two DDD tits . . .

Eric: Wow.

Cameryn: I certainly don't get any complaints! Let's see . . . I have a nice round ass to match, so I'm a little bit of an hourglass.

Eric: Mmmm.

Cameryn: Ha ha, I can tell what you'd be looking at if I walked into your room right now! . . . I've got long legs. Short, wavy, dark blonde hair, and blue eyes. And I've been around the block a little bit, so anything you want to throw at me, I can catch it and run with it.

Eric: You sound amazing.

What's a nice girl to do when she doesn't have the time to talk dirty? Perhaps the most common obstacle I hear is an imbalance of too much stress and too little time. After all, intimacy education and support can go only so far when you barely have time to wave at each other, much less exchange a kiss. How will you ever find a private moment to practice flirting?

As widespread as this complaint is, the paths to resolving it are fairly simple. What's tough is convincing people that these techniques work and are worthwhile to develop. It seems too easy, too good to be true, but improving how we treat ourselves and our relationships mindfully actually makes the rest of our commitments smoother, pleasanter, and easier to resolve.

Better life balance isn't the answer to everything, but it's an essential foundation to improving our relationships. I'm not talking about being "perfect" at everything, with a baby bottle in one hand and your most fashionable handbag in the other, and sexy lingerie underneath your business attire. Far from it! I'm more interested in encouraging you to let yourself be less perfect in the name of a bit of fun and flirtation. I've got the real-life proof that it can work for you, and learning to talk dirty can be your key to some amazing relational and personal changes.

It's easy to sell a nice girl on the importance of self-care as long as the focus isn't on her. How can we do our best for our careers, our children, our relationships, our families, and our volunteer efforts if we're worn-out and world-weary? Clearly we must take good care of ourselves so that we can continue to have the energy to make life better for the ones we love. But I want to take the rationale for self-care a step further than that. You should also take good care of yourself because you deserve it, unconditionally.

You're Worth It

Stay with me here. I do believe that it's important to keep ourselves in good condition so that we can be well-oiled machines, but there's so much more to us than that. We also deserve a happy, healthy, and pleasurable life. After all, how can we truly enjoy our relationships if we're not feeling good about our own quality of life and our sensuality as women? How can we experience the love lives we long for when we barely have the time and energy to find matching socks for everyone in the house? Perhaps our sexual and personal self-care should begin to take a bit more priority than those socks.

Don't believe me? Ask Trinity, one of my former students. I met Trinity while she was wrapping up the last semester of her course work to become a therapist. Not only had she returned to school for a graduate degree, she was also working full-time and planning her wedding. In-laws, financial surprises, health problems, dresses, relational stress, and all manner of other concerns popped up along the way, as they do in times like these.

Trinity mentioned to me that she was worried about her ability to pass her classes and was thinking of taking a leave of absence from school, with no idea when she might return. This dynamic, intelligent, beautiful, and caring woman had put her own needs on the back burner to such an extent that she was facing the very real possibility of giving up on her academic program mere weeks before graduation! I could only imagine what this may have been doing to her personal life, too.

We spoke at length, sometimes by phone and sometimes by e-mail. Together, we concocted a truly counterintuitive plan of attack: She would stop working, planning, and responding to her other tasks by early evening each night. Her duties wouldn't stop asking for her time then, but she would learn to politely decline or direct them to other resources. Not only that, she decided to take it a giant leap further and declared that she deserved an hour or two of self-pampering right smack in the middle of every day! To be honest with you, I wasn't sure if she was biting off more than she could chew, but it was worth a try.

And so Trinity's letters and calls began to change. It was tough at first, and she often felt guilty about spending time on pedicures, taking naps, and catching up on her reading. Soon she was adding daily walks, time with her girlfriends, and extra snuggles with her honey. She began to share stories of her increasingly frequent (and fun) date nights, and it didn't take long before she began to look forward to caring for herself and her sensual side more and more.

An interesting thing happened along the way, she noticed. Eventually her job learned to stop turning to her for every little thing that needed to be done after-hours. Her sweetie enjoyed their relaxed time together, and he began picking up more tasks around the house to help make that possible, and she learned to let him even though he didn't always do things just as she would like. And I saw her high grades hold steady even though she confessed that she wasn't spending as much time on homework as she had before.

Her life had shifted focus during her grand, unconventional experiment. Instead of basing her schedule around her to-do list and fitting in joy now and then, she did what she needed to do quickly and with renewed energy as she kept her eye on her time spent enjoying life. What a sensual and seductive way to live! Who wouldn't be attracted to someone with such an enticing balance of competency and frolicking fun? I'm pleased to report that Trinity graduated on time and had a beautiful wedding. Although she still has to remind herself that she really can slow down without falling behind, she's so grateful that she learned how to create better balance in her life and relationship.

Trinity isn't the only example of the magic of prioritizing ourselves simply because we deserve it, with wonderful consequences in other areas of life. I recently met Blake and Cornell, a charming couple who had all but forgotten how to sexually connect as they once had because of the stress of day-to-day life. One night, over a glass of wine, Blake laughingly suggested that they have sex every night for the next month. To her surprise, Cornell agreed to the challenge, and they set up a calendar to keep track of their successes. Suddenly, sexual interaction leapt to the top of their to-do list, with neither wanting to let the other down.

Blake told me that she was amazed by what happened when they both decided to see their love life as a priority; other obligations stepped to the side to make way, without any negative repercussions. Arguments, e-mail, television shows, and even some housekeeping duties diminished in importance, but nothing fell apart. In fact, life had become far better, and their relationship was blooming again.

Making Time for Pleasure

Making the time and space for sex and pleasure doesn't always come naturally, no matter how much we think it should or wish it would. It took support, dedication, and teamwork for Trinity, Blake, Cornell, and every one of my other clients to learn to make room for themselves and their relationships, but each of them was able to do it with positive results. As these people learned, the first step to making time and energy for sensuality is to recognize that we can't count on nature to take over and fix our sexual struggles. Sure, there may have been a time when hormones or carefree youth allowed that to be the case, but real life has kicked in since then. With our days, weeks, and months either scheduled down to the minute or spent in rushed chaos, it's essential that we make room to nurture our sensual selves.

To create this change, we must also be able to talk it over with ourselves and our sweeties. When it comes to giving my clients homework, I prefer to assign fun tasks that allow them to help me explore things that might create change for them. Every one of my clients has discovered that nothing kills the mood faster than an angry or desperate conversation about how their sex life is dead and they can barely remember what their partner looks like nude anymore, unless it's during a mad rush to get dressed in the morning.

At the core of those laments is a collection of common themes that I work to help them encounter. With a little practice, anyone can learn to turn offending complaints into sensual invitations for sexy solutions. Instead of flinging accusations, it's far more fun and effective to invite each other to team up on the tasks at hand so you can enjoy celebrating together afterward as a strong, sexy team!

The suggestion of scheduled dates has been offered so frequently by relationship experts and television sitcoms that it's become trite. It sounds so simple and clear, but the "date night" advice holds little value without a solid understanding of the underpinnings of the concept. When we add ourselves and our relationships to our planner (in ink, not pencil) we're telling ourselves something rare and important: We're just as essential as the most urgent appointment on the calendar.

Stop for a moment to let that soak in: Nothing in your life is more important than your well-being and that of your family, including your relationship. Likewise, nothing should be more important to your partner than their well-being and relationship with you (and your children, if you're parents). Isn't that joy, comfort, and security what you're working so hard for, anyway?

Stop waiting for that moment when you'll finally be free to enjoy it. Embrace your seductive energy right now. Lower your book for a moment and blow a kiss or send a loving text message to your main squeeze. You're in this life journey together, and you have every right and reason to enjoy each other every step of the way!

We discovered earlier that scheduled romantic time only works if we understand that it's possible and why it's important. We know that even the busiest women and couples can make time to get frisky when they make it a priority. We also have you thinking about the fact that you're worth the time and energy to enjoy your sensual, playful side. But what about spontaneity? Isn't that the heart of seduction and excitement? How can we be spontaneous with our calendars pulled up on our smart phones?

Love Requires Dedication

Several years ago one of my good friends, Ji-Hyun, a delightful family therapist, shared a discovery with me. First, though, she tested it out on me by calling and asking why I'm still with my spouse. This is the sort of thing relationship experts talk about when we get together, so the question didn't seem odd to me at all. I offered a long list of reasons, including positive attributes of my sweetie, ways in which he brings out the best in me, things we have in common, challenges we had successfully faced together or that taught us how to do things better in the future, and finally I mentioned that I'm also deeply in love with him.

She then shared this reflection with me: She'd seen only troubled couples list love as the first reason. Individuals and couples in solid partnerships mentioned it at the very end of their list, or not at all. On deeper reflection, I realized that the same thing was often true of the clients in my relationship coaching and education practices. It wasn't because the people in more solid relationships valued love any less, or were any less in love with each other. They simply realized that love was not enough to make a relationship work, while those in struggling relationships dearly wished that their love could be powerful enough to yield solutions to their relational woes.

A deep, loving bond in a modern relationship is akin to having a door to enter your home. You hardly notice your front door unless it needs repair (or somehow goes missing), at which point you can't stop thinking about how important it is. Love is as vital to your relationship as an exterior door is to your home, yet it takes far more than love to make life enjoyable and successful. Dedication and attentiveness are foremost on the list of requirements to get the most out of your partnership and your life!

Yearning for spontaneity is another trap. If we dig beneath the surface of our cultural insistence on erotic spontaneity, we'll quickly find that we're facing that same, destructive core myth of sex: Everything about it should come naturally. It's the wish for some magical force to come and make it right for us. Whether it's an irresistible knight in shining armor (with a nice haircut, flush bank account, and generous personality) or a sexy lover who whisks you away on an unplanned dinner date then returns you to a clean house for some passionate lovemaking, fantasies of spontaneity certainly are enticing.

There's no reason to give up these fantasies, but if you want them to come true then you'll need to open the door and set the stage just a bit. Just like everything else in love and life, a little bit of planning can lead to some enjoyable results! To get in the proper mind-set, I suggest you remind yourself that any relationship is an example of how two become three when they fall in love. That's right, I said three.

A delightfully rich interconnection is woven when we find ourselves in a relationship with a new partner. While we've heard the old line about two becoming one many times, this loving sexual imagery fails to capture the complexity of couples. It would be more accurate, instead, to say that a new entity is born when the two come together: that of the relationship itself. Now there are always three of you, especially when the two of you are alone.

Keeping this in mind, as well as what your obligations are to each party, can help illuminate new ways to make time, space, and motivation for verbal seduction and all of the delicious activities it will yield. You, your partner, and the relationship all require nurturance and effort to keep things running smoothly and happily for all involved. Let's explore how to help make that happen.

Partners and Teammates

The term *partner* is useful not only for degendering the conversation and handling moments when you're unsure of a couple's official status but also for invoking the concept of teamwork. Partners, teammates, lovers: This powerful unity takes on a life of its own in stable relationships. When a romantic partnership is pained and acting up, the wounded relational-entity is begging for much-needed care and attention. It takes a capable, skilled, and upbeat team to care for a relationship!

To be a strong teammate, we must be responsible for our own holistic well-being so that we can bring our best selves to the effort. Every personal issue that's put on the back burner still takes up space, energy, and attention to keep it from burning to the bottom of the pan. Bringing those concerns to the front burner to finish them, handing them off to another chef, or simply tossing them out and washing the pot is essential.

What have you left on the back burner far too long, and what can you do to get it off the stove? Who needs to know about the situation and who can you enlist to help? You're responsible for utilizing your resources, including your sweetie, to identify and tackle the things that are holding you back and stressing you out. It's your partner's task to hear you and offer the help, whether that's attentive support or active assistance. As you continue to take charge of communicating and advocating for your own well-being, and recruiting effective help in that effort, you become a stronger teammate.

Your partners have the same obligation to themselves, including the task of communicating their needs to you. The exchange of assistance should be mutual and end up making lighter work for everyone. It's the emotional equivalent of putting the most assertive, smooth-talking partner in charge of calling the credit card company while the introverted planner takes over making a better payment schedule for the household's bills. Neither task is particularly pleasant, but matching tasks with natural talent results in a better resolution for everyone involved. It's each person's responsibility to ensure that neither of you is backing away from the need to communicate nor using it as an excuse to dump responsibilities on the other.

Finally, it's the relationship's job to inspire, provide support, and contribute joy and solidarity to both of you. You and your partner are there to provide the support team to nurture the relationship so that it can keep doing its job. Your relationship lives in the invisible spaces between you and your partner, forming an essential triangle of interpersonal connection. Often it's women who are most highly attuned to the health of the relational-entity, as well as that of their partners and children. Ironically, nice girls are also most likely to push awareness of their own status to the back of their minds.

This isn't to say that every woman is a relationship-psychic or that men are the interpersonal bumblers of the world. Your relationship, regardless of the genders involved and who minds the health of the partnership, most likely contains at least one person who's tuned into this aspect. This is an essential quality, if we listen to our senses, communicate our intuition, and have partners who value this input.

Liz and Martin were a particularly striking example of what happens when we forget that two become three. Love simply wasn't enough to buoy the relationship through their current struggles; they needed to face their stressors as a team. I asked for what they hoped to accomplish with me, their goals for the relationship.

As often happens, they responded with a significant list of complaints and worries that seemed to multiply as they spoke. Sometimes they worked together to describe a problem, other times they turned to me with their invisible fingers pointed squarely at each other to declare what each needed and how the other fell short. All the while, their body language communicated shared passion as well as despair; this relationship was not dead yet, but it was bleeding badly and needed prompt attention.

Liz was on her third tissue and Martin had his arms crossed in a posture of anxious self-protection when they finally paused to rack their brains for any other problems. To their surprise, I rose from my chair and settled into a cross-legged position on the floor. I explained that I was creating a seat for the person they kept forgetting, the one who hadn't yet had a chance to voice its needs: their relationship.

After a bit of laughter about the new arrangement, I explained the idea of two becoming three and asked them to each consider what they knew about their relationship. I suggested that many of their concerns were symptoms of illness and injury in their relationship, as well as hurdles to each person's ability to respond to it. Slowly, I guided them to refocus on the relationship and what it needed, as well as what each of them needed to work on as a team to heal and preserve the relationship.

There was a prompt and dramatic change as they began a new list. Liz noted that to attend to the relationship she needed to feel like a social priority to Martin, but she also needed to diversify her own social resources. Martin quietly noted that he could tune into the relationship better if he took care of his own health better, including cutting back on his recent increase in drinking. That would allow him to increase the quality of his time with Liz and also make it easier for him to be aware of his own needs. They discussed how they could help each other with their individual goals and how they could each contribute to the health of the relationship. By the end, their hands were clasped while they spoke, their toes were side by side, and I had the feeling that they were headed home for a bit of stress-relieving and bonding intimacy.

It takes time and effort to prioritize sex and romance. It would be a grave disservice for me to lead you to believe that learning to talk dirty is a magical elixir for an ailing relationship, the oral equivalent of your partnership's knight in shining armor. You and I both know that isn't true, no matter how lovely it would be if it were.

What dirty talk can do is help us have hot, steamy fun while we discover and disclose our naughtiest desires. It's a dynamic communication skill for our sexual needs, our relationship pleasures, and our appreciation for the best in our lovers. The art of talking dirty, when applied to a relationship that's ready for it, can take both of you to exciting and nurturing levels of interpersonal connection and bliss.

Key Points

- Making time and space for pleasure is essential to be able to enjoy your sexuality.
- You must believe that you deserve to feel pleasure and enjoy your own sexual energy first; otherwise, your efforts will fall flat or feel hollow.
- Many couples' complaints are grounded in real and legitimate needs that could be expressed in more inviting and proactive ways. Instead of struggling with negative energy, focus on becoming a team in which you nurture yourselves (and each other) as well as the relationship itself.

EXERCISE

What's one small but essential change that would help you better enjoy your sexual energy, either alone or with a sweetie? Take a moment to write it down as concisely and clearly as possible. Then consider how you might propose this change as an enticing invitation, instead of an accusation of deficiency. Take a moment to write that down, too. If you feel ready, use a little sexy language. If you're not ready for that yet, keep reading!

THREE

Become a Secret Erotic Superhero

Cameryn: Well, I have a good time . . . So. You like the look of my ass, huh?

Eric: Oh, yeah.

Cameryn: Or is it my pussy you want?

Eric: Your pussy. I would love to eat that all night.

Cameryn: So you say. But I want to know how hungry you are. I'm gonna walk in the room and sit down on a chair across from you, my long legs open wide and my skirt riding up slightly above my knees. You're looking, aren't you . . . ?

Eric: Yes.

Most of my clients approach me for accurate sexual information, better relational balance, and sexual enhancement that fits into their busy lives and specific needs. I'm still searching for my orgasms, and I could use a little help finding them. What happened to our love life, and how do we get it back or fire it up? How can I reclaim my sexuality after all I've been through? How do I talk with my partner about sexual needs or concerns? I'm not even sure what turns me on; how do I find out and then share my to-do list? Things just haven't been the same since menopause, chemo, the baby, the divorce, or the surgery . . .

Despite building a career out of sex and intimacy outreach, I have a special place in my heart for folks who don't base their lives around the erotic but do recognize that it's still an important part of individual and relational balance. I call these my secretly daring clients, and if you think of yourself the same way (or want to), then you're in good company.

The Secretly Daring Woman

Secretly daring women love a bit of spicy fantasy, but they don't want to give their lives over to it, at least not for too long. If you're secretly daring, then you appreciate the way a sexy piece of negligee makes you swing your hips, especially if it doesn't need to be dry-cleaned. A nice girl can be secretly daring when she's in the mood, once she's discovered the fun of releasing her inner vixen.

For some nice girls, being a bit naughty (privately or even publicly) is an especially exciting way to be nice to themselves, their relationships, and the lucky subjects of their desire. Indeed, there are as many ways to be a nice girl as there are women who consider themselves such! What we have in common is a desire to create balance in our lives and relationships, combining our astounding ability to blend daily tasks with an exciting sparkle of the exotic.

Remember the classic Superman comics where Clark Kent wore his glasses and proper tie, and no one knew beneath that button-down shirt lay an amazing set of abs and the ability to stop a speeding train with his bare hands? I like to think of nice girls as the sexual female equivalent. For some women, their secret superhero status is so well hidden that they're not even aware of it, and their lovers may be the first to know. Finch told me about his erotic superhero wife who has yet to realize her amazing powers: "When she feels confident and is in the mood to go upstairs I'm just in awe of her, of her face and her body. I wish I could tell her how she looks to me right then, how everything about her is pure sex, but it would only make her self-conscious and shy. I wish she knew how hot she is when she turns it on and turns me on." Other women suspect that they just might have erotic superhero powers yet to be discovered, if they could only figure out how to find them.

What does it take for a nice girl to discover (or develop) her own secret identity as an irresistible vixen, able to leap self-doubts and a busy schedule in a single bound? It begins with an honest inventory of what stands in your way right now.

It Starts with Honesty

Granita shared her thoughts while talking about her newly discovered lust for talking dirty during sex.

> *For me, I had to commit myself to being truly honest about sex in my relationship. It was a little scary. Actually, it was very scary to realize that I had become so good at playing along with sex that I didn't even realize I was faking it. My moans were on autopilot and I didn't bother to try to have real orgasms with him. Now that I've decided to learn what I like and stop shaping myself to his pleasure, I'm a lot more vulnerable, and I'm discovering that sex can be so much better. Now I'm working on how to balance my pleasure with his in different situations. Recently I noticed that I've started responding by telling him how things feel and what I like, and it's gotten really fun and dirty for both of us! It's hot.*

For Granita, her sexual stumbling blocks came in the form of self-awareness and sexual honesty. Once she realized this and began to tackle those issues, she found herself free to be vulnerable and increase her seductiveness right along with her enjoyment.

"I just didn't grow up that way," commented Jess over a cup of tea:

> *Maybe it's when I was born or where I was raised, but that's just not how it was. When I had my bachelorette party, which was very mild, one of my girlfriends gave me a box of panty liners and whispered that I might discover some 'uncomfortable discharge' after my first time. That might have been the most explicit any of my friends were about the details of having sex. Of course I thanked her and never let on that I had been sexually active with my boyfriends for years. That just isn't the sort of thing we talk about with our girlfriends or our men. How in the world could someone like me ever tell a man how to touch me, much less enjoy talking dirty like that? He would probably fall out of the bed in shock if I did. I'm not sure I even want to know if he likes that sort of thing.*

Jess had very specific ideas of what it means for a woman to be sexually assertive, as well as what sexual assertiveness looks like. For her, being a nice girl is governed by strict social rules about sex and gender. While some of these rules have a valuable place in our lives, some of them simply aren't designed for our benefit. Jess's stumbling blocks could be addressed by restructuring the private rules of sexuality and relationships in her life so that they serve her (and her partners) more effectively. On top of that, Jess could also consider different ways to express herself that don't feel "dirty" while still improving sexual communication. There are many different styles of dirty talk, many of which are quite sweet! Who knows which she'll like best once she begins to explore?

Remember Shawna, from Chapter One, who laid back and waited for the men in her life to take the initiative and make sex happen however they liked? Her most caring lovers tried unsuccessfully to read her mind, while the others decided that they simply couldn't be bothered to consider her pleasure. Sure, Shawna enjoyed many things about sex and sometimes it was quite pleasurable, but it was always focused on her partner's interests (whether in themselves or in her), and orgasms were rare.

"Orgasms aren't that important to me," she conceded. Indeed, many women have shared that feeling with me, and there's nothing wrong with defining sexual success as far more diverse than orgasms. The problem occurs when we're the only one in the relationship going without and smiling about it, when it stems from experiences that led us to believe that we don't orgasm readily or conveniently enough (or at all), or some of each. For Shawna,

> It would be unimaginable for me to orgasm as often as he does now. I mean, that would be almost every time we have sex plus all of the times I get him off between times when we have sex. Seriously, I can't imagine it, especially if he only orgasmed when I do now, by myself after he falls asleep or not at all. I'm fine like this. I mean, this is just how it is, so why start trouble or make an issue of it? It's fine, really. I like sex, and I get a lot of other things out of it.

Shawna has fantastic erotic superhero potential; she loves to flirt for hours and can be just as tempting on the phone or online as she is in person. She has confidence in her skills with pleasing her partners, but she can't help admitting that she loves "the fantasy of someone who just knows how to work it right, who can figure my body out as well as I have."

Rescuing Our Own Sexuality

For Shawna, her stumbling blocks revolve around the popular fantasy of a sexual knight in shining armor (or perhaps glowing amour), who gallops up to sweep her off to a life of pleasure with his mighty sword. The princess pays her dues before his arrival, and then is treated to the opportunity to let someone take over responsibility for her romantic and personal well-being. In the stories, it's always worthwhile for her to sacrifice self-sufficiency for a whole new world of love.

Most women, including Shawna, wave this fantasy away with disdain. As modern women, we know better than to expect a man to save us from anything, and our celebrity gossip blogs tell us that even when it happens it doesn't result in happily ever after. We expect to work hard in all areas of life and strive to reap the rewards of our effort in the form of professional and domestic happiness and security.

But, for some reason, when it comes to sex, many women are still stuck dreaming of the fantasy prince with the magic sword. Since we know he isn't real, many of us simply decide to lower our expectations: Good enough for us forms around what's good enough for him, at least when it comes to seduction and sexual pleasure. We just hope we're in there somewhere.

It's time to wake up, ladies. We know that the prince isn't coming to whisk us away from our daily stress, so let's let go of the hope that he's coming to our bedrooms, too. Frankly, I heard from some reliable sources that he's kind of a jerk, anyway. It's no loss, because something far better awaits us.

By taking responsibility for becoming experts on our own bodies, pleasure, orgasms, and arousal, we can find our way to far better sex lives. It takes work, but we're no strangers to effort. Now we're simply dedicating that effort to our own sexual well-being. Let go of those tired old lies about the complexity and difficulty of female pleasure—they simply exist to cover up a lack of self-understanding and sexual savvy. We now have access to a wealth of information and professionals to help us catch up on that missing knowledge.

The next step is to raise our expectations for our relationships by developing confident sexual communication skills and settling for nothing less than a lover who's eager to be our teammate in pleasure, both theirs and ours. Replace the hope for a mind reader (it was never fair of us to begin with) with that of a partner who longs to learn how to read our body language. Exploring together helps build the intimacy of our relationship.

No doubt you've heard the truism that confidence is the sexiest thing a woman can wear, so cover yourself in it and shoo away anyone who isn't seduced by your hard-earned glow. Instead of being a sexually helpless princess-wannabe, lying quietly on unsullied satin sheets, you can develop your sexual muscles (literally and metaphorically) and become your own erotic superhero! Who needs a spoiled knight when you can start a speeding orgasm with your own bare hands and show a lover how you like it? And if you miss that knight's mighty sword, you can always buy a few for your bedside table and invite your lovers to explore them with you.

While some might fear that taking responsibility for your own sexual well-being and standards is unattractive or brash, it's actually downright romantic! Unleashing your true romantic can be one of your mightiest superpowers. That's right, it's nothing short of hot and sexy when a lover of any gender coyly offers ideas that enhance everyone's evenings.

The Power of Seduction

Being able to switch who takes charge of intimate exchanges allows both of you some escape from the beast of performance anxiety, whether we're talking about flirting or touching. You're a team with the goal of having a good time, and you have each other's back. And front!

The first step in successfully romancing a partner is making them feel special, and right on its heels is offering a tantalizing promise of intimacy and pleasure to come. An erotic super-hero's confidence makes the object of our attention know they must be something special to catch our eye, even (especially) if they've been catching our eye for a few decades now.

And once our love realizes what a fortunate position they're in, they should be quick to recognize that we have the ability and desire to share an exquisite interlude with them. Who wouldn't love to be captured by powers like those? It's even better when we can combine those powers by nurturing and complementing our partner's romantic style, so we can really rock our relationship as a team!

When we seduce our partners, we also have the opportunity to seduce ourselves. In fact, seducing ourselves can be a powerful aphrodisiac for our partners all by itself! Instead of focusing all of our skills of enticement on what we know our partners enjoy, we can change our approach a bit, to our benefit and theirs. While there's certainly a selfish aspect to all of this self-sufficient superhero talk, when done well it can be in perfect balance with attributes of intimacy and nurturing within a relationship.

There's no need to choose between being a giving lover and a confident, self-indulgent lover. There's room for both, and they can happen simultaneously. A caring partner enjoys their partner's pleasure, and enjoys sharing their own pleasure with their partner just as much. A healthy sense of confidence doesn't leave anyone out, except those who simply aren't inter-ested in meeting reasonable romantic standards.

Envisioning yourself as an erotic superhero may be a whole new story of who you are, a completely foreign plot for your life. Don't let that stop you! This book called to you, or the person who thought of you when they saw it, for a reason. A door has cracked open, and no matter what your past chapters have included, you have the opportunity to write in an enticing new side of yourself.

I suspect, though, that there have been hints and foreshadowing all the way. When we think of who we are, or try to describe our identity, we choose certain aspects from our pasts for inclusion and edit out the rest. If we think of ourselves as safe drivers, we're probably crossing out that incident with the ticket as an exception. If we consider ourselves smart, then we aren't counting those few moments when we messed up an obvious task, because those aren't representative of who we are. Science backs this up and shows us how valuable it is to have this automatic editing function as a part of our identity.

Research shows that when things go wrong for folks with good self-esteem, they're more likely to blame outside forces and continue rolling along to later successes. But depressed individuals are much more likely to blame themselves even if it wasn't their fault, wasting unnecessary time and energy on building a story of themselves rooted in their depression. In other words, when we have a positive story of ourselves and who we are, we find ways to add enjoyable accounts and attributes to every chapter of our lives, and the reverse is also true. It's not so much about the occurrences in our lives but about how we view them and which events we decide to include in our stories of our identity.

Some models of therapy, especially narrative therapy, build their approach on this knowledge about people and focus on helping their clients to comb back through the events of their lives to build new plots and concepts of who they are out of parts of their lives previously edited out. They help their clients to build success stories by making the positive "exceptions" the highlights. You can do the same for your own concept of your sexual self!

For every event or action in your life, there's a matching meaning. Is your interest in this book chance, curiosity, a last-ditch effort, or evidence of your own ability to let loose your secret erotic superhero? I believe wholeheartedly that every one of us can move toward healthier, happier sexual well-being, regardless of our pasts. We can each write, rewrite, and edit our own sexual stories to include self-confidence and powerful intimacy.

Key Points

- Every nice girl can enjoy a secret identity as a sexual superhero who inspires and energizes her throughout her love life as well as more mundane activities.
- Taking control of our sexual selves by understanding what we want and need, and how to ask for it, is essential to a pleasurable sex life. There's nothing inappropriate or unexciting about being sexually aware and assertive!
- Sometimes being sexually honest with yourself is the most challenging task, yet it's one of the most important steps that you can make toward living a more fulfilling and pleasure-filled life.

EXERCISE

What does sexual pleasure mean to you, and what role does it play in your life? Take a moment to consider these questions, and whether you really know the answer yet. They're questions worth pondering. If you can, ask some of your closest friends the same questions and listen to their answers. Once you have some ideas about how you'd answer them, compare your answers with what you'd like them to be. What would it take for you to bridge the gap between where you are and where you'd like to be? Finally, write a sensually worded letter to yourself, inviting yourself to take a first step toward these changes and giving yourself full permission to enjoy the transition.

FOUR

Discover Your Style

Cameryn: I know you want a look up my skirt. The way you're sitting there on the edge of the chair and shaking. You can practically see the heat rising from me. I raise my skirt higher and slide down lower in the easy chair. See it?

Eric: Are you hairy?

Cameryn: Yes, baby. Can't you see it? The curly dark-blonde hair, the deep pink lips, the pale skin of my tender inner thighs. You can almost smell it, if you could just get closer. You want to get closer?

Eric: Please!

Close your eyes and imagine the ultimate dirty-talking woman. What does she look like, where is she, who is she with, and what is she doing? By the end of this book, I hope that you'll be envisioning yourself verbalizing your most enticing, private turn-ons with your sweethearts. But right now, most of us probably have a different image in mind.

When I pose this question to my clients and workshop participants, they often imagine a rough-edged phone-sex operator, complete with cigarette and either hair curlers or stilettos. Other images that top the list include intoxicated sorority girls with a football team's worth of sexual experience, a savvy and firm professional dominatrix, or a demanding yet wanton perfectionist of a CEO with a jones for underlings who work late.

While all of these can make for stimulating fantasy fodder, few of us ladies identify with such images daily. Only fierce, demanding, greedy, or sexually detached women are perceived as accomplished dirty talkers. Men don't fare well, either; most people imagined a park flasher, womanizing frat boy, or unpleasant ex-boyfriend when asked what a dirty-talking man looks like. Dirty talkers of the world definitely need a style makeover and a better marketing department. It's time to redefine who gets to talk dirty, when, why, and how!

Let me assure you that dirty talkers do take the above forms, but that's far from the end of the story. Those stereotypes are the vast minority of lovers (and professionals) offering scintillating whispers in the darkened corners of posh restaurants. Whether in stilettos, cowboy boots, sneakers, or barefoot, women from every layer of society are letting wanton enticements slip from their lips. It's a rather exciting notion, if you give it some thought.

You're in Good Company

As quiet and guarded as we may be about our sexuality in casual conversation, we're surrounded by secret examples of how dynamic and common it is to share our desires. The woman on the bus, hair tucked in a uniform cap on the way to work: Can you be sure of what she's texting and to whom? How about the parking attendant who just closed her phone, or the soccer mom who leaned over to say something to her cheering spouse?

How would we see the world differently if we could listen in on these private conversations, even for just a moment? We'd surely realize that there's nothing unusual, shameful, or inappropriate about discovering and expressing our desires. We'd also see just how many different women have discovered the art of talking dirty, blowing away any preconceived notions about the kind of women who do that. It's comforting to know that we're in good company when we want to talk dirty, and it also opens up a world of possibilities for when and how we do it. We can invoke a world of fantasies with our words, like all those dirty talk stereotypes, but we can also tap into our own feminine sexuality and power as a nice girl, an intelligent girl, or however we see ourselves.

Dirty talk can be sensual, sassy, corruptible, nerdy, experienced, sweet, and more. It's far more dynamic (and better) than just coming up with a long list of downright nasty words. Such blue language may not even fit your personal style of aural seduction, but that doesn't mean you can't be irresistibly seductive! An almost-innocent turn of phrase can become an unforgettable erotic moment for any lover. To begin building your vocabulary and confidence, let's start by finding a style that works for you.

Going Beyond Dirty Words

When women come to me asking for help with dirty talking, they usually begin by claiming that they don't know enough explicit language or how to use it. Most of the time (with plenty of exceptions) boyfriends and husbands have prompted them to be more verbal, more direct, or simply more sexual. They're on the phone with me in hopes of being a better lover for their men.

It's a noble quest, assuming he's just as proactive about improving himself. But in most situations it becomes clear that she could find a list of dirty words or sample scripts online and fix the problem without me if it were that simple. Deep down, she wants something else. She wants to be that persona he's seeking to evoke in her, instead of just pretending to be.

Dirty talk should flow authentically from the heart and loins, not just from your old high school drama classes. A flair for a bit of role-play is a phenomenal tool, but without grounding in your authentic, sexual self, it won't feel right. Eventually it'll become stale and repetitive as you struggle for new scripts that sound hotter than you feel. We'll get to those vocabulary tricks and lists later, but first let's make sure that you're learning how to tap into your real, sexy self instead of limiting your opportunities for joy to what you think someone else wants to hear.

Raise your book (paper or digital) and block out the world around you for a moment. Take a deep breath and remember the last time that you felt incredibly, glowingly confident. It probably wasn't a particularly erotic moment, although those certainly count! Perhaps someone complimented your child, indirectly giving you some overdue praise as a parent. How about that presentation that made your employees and boss beam, or when you finally figured out that home improvement project? Maybe it was the way you felt as you slid into those amazing shoes, the pair that match your favorite cocktail dress perfectly, and strutted your way into a fantastic night out.

Take a moment to focus on one time when you felt truly confident, solidly powerful in your female energy, and maybe even in your sexual energy. Remember where you were, the sounds around you, what you were doing, and how you were dressed. Don't stop recalling the details until you have a solid grin on your face, beaming behind your book. We'll spend this chapter working on developing a confident moment into a sexy style, but if you need a quick review for this skill later, you can also turn to the "Find Your Confident Moment" activity directions in Chapter 12.

Before I go any farther, I want to acknowledge that you might not be able to think of such a proud, confident moment. We're rarely encouraged to recount or be bold about our successes, much less to dwell on them until we smile at our own aptitude and accomplishments. Bragging, gloating, taking undue praise, or simply being snobby are activities no one wants to be known for. Right now, though, you have permission to put yourself on the highest pedestal you can find, risk-free. In fact, if you find it difficult to identify a confident moment, it may be that you've fallen into a habit of being too humble for your own good. Sexiness, including dirty talk, requires as much confidence as it does humor to work well. We can't know what we want and communicate it well to others if we don't feel that we deserve anything special, whether it's in bed, in the kitchen, or in the office.

There's nothing wrong with you if you've learned to be overly humble. Lots of societal forces encourage you to be so, and humbleness certainly has its benefits. Every time I work with groups of women to find their sexy, dirty talking styles, at least one woman struggles to connect with a confident moment. Sometimes most of the women in attendance find it difficult, and it's often a shock to realize how hard it is.

If you identify with this struggle to find a confident moment, it simply means that it's time to develop a new habit of balancing your humble side with the credit you deserve, and the chutzpah to let it inspire you in delightful ways. Before we go any farther into developing your dirty talk style, let's make sure you know exactly how much you deserve to show (and feel) your swagger. You may wish to skip ahead to Chapter 11 and read about Lena and Dorian, a couple who learned to work together to highlight how incredible each of them is and how much they appreciate each other.

Once you've settled on a confident moment and brought enough vivid detail and context to it that you can visualize the memory and almost feel as though you're there now, you hold the key to your first dirty talk style. There'll be many more in your future, but you deserve some strong inspiration to start you on solid ground. How would you describe yourself during this confident moment? Consider adjectives like sweet, sassy, devil-may-care, direct, savvy, deceptive, active, pampered, and so on. This is an important step, so take the time to write up a list of at least five such words. Ten would be even better. If you struggle to reach that number, pull up an online thesaurus or find one on your bookshelf.

Your list should be the sort of description that would inspire a comic-book artist to create a new hero (an erotic superhero, when she chooses to be) with an attitude and presentation just like yours in that moment. This rich, honest, and dynamic facet of yourself is now prepped and ready to set the stage.

While your confident moment may not have been a sexual one, it was still connected to your sacred, female energy. You can shape that into sexual energy at your will. Forget all those stereotypes about dirty talkers from the beginning of the chapter. This is a real seductress, and I can practically see the heat emanating from her.

To get you started, I'd like to share a few stories of my favorite aural seductresses. Every one of them is a real woman, and a few are blends of friends with similar styles. Some of these stories will remind you of yourself, and others will not. Grab a pen and note the parts that grab your attention and resemble you, and then jot down how it could be an even better fit.

The Sweet Talker

My dear friend Ellie is the sweetest seductress I've ever met. It's clear to everyone she passes when she's having a confident day; you can't help but feel it when she speaks or even smiles. Men approach her constantly (and usually respectfully) regardless of whether she's the thinnest, best-dressed, most feminine, or most flirtatious woman in our group. I can't imagine an ounce of dirty vamp in her, but that doesn't stop her from treating her lovers to delightfully dirty words.

I remember standing next to her in a New England coffee shop. She wore a pair of brown European clogs with cute stitching, a bulky gray sweater over a long-sleeved cotton T, and yoga pants. Her straight, brown hair was tossed quickly into a clip, the only color on her face from the all-natural, tinted gloss on her confident smile. Ellie was dressed to be the kind of local you would trust for directions if you were a tourist, or show off to your friends over a game of darts at the pub if you were her sweetie.

We stood there browsing the bakery case and chatting about tomorrow's day trip to New York City as the barista approached. Young and handsome in a purposely carefree way, and clearly smitten, he asked if he could help us. More accurately, he asked her if we were ready as I grinned and watched her work her effortless brand of magic.

Looking up, she beamed at him and issued a "thank you" that would make chocolate melt on a winter night in the tundra! It wasn't just appreciation. The tone of her voice carried an undertone of desire, her full attention, and a slight suggestion of flirtation. It was as comfortable as her shoes, and just as mindfully chosen. It was subtle, yet unmissable. Just like that, he was hers until we left the shop, his number in her pocket.

Her dirty talk with him started with a simple, authentic statement, no lewdness needed. Of course, their private murmurs would be less suitable for a public audience. They'd still be just as honest, just as real as she is. Ellie's confidence can best be described as intimate, and she's my favorite sweet talker. Every partner feels like he's the only one, the most important, and also the luckiest man alive. She enjoys playful erotic language, constructive feedback during lovemaking, and laughter mixed with her moans.

Some of her most confident moments involve intelligent, creative activities such as painting, conducting and presenting research, and mentoring students. She brings these same touches to how she combines language with her sex life. Sweet talkers are unintimidating yet no less powerful when they decide to share their sexual energy, and are imbued with an incredible, yet comfortable, erotic magnetism.

The Direct Talker

For every bit of easy sweetness that Ellie exudes, Rochelle replaces it with directness. She's no-nonsense and takes a great deal of joy in discovering what gives her pleasure; she plays as hard as she works. Rochelle is definitely a direct talker, and while her conversation flows in fast and energetic words, her dirty talk is paced and pointed with lots of eye contact.

She feels most confident in her black, unisex, designer cowboy boots and onyx liquid eyeliner. She prefers leadership positions and values a good follower as much as the opportunity to speak in public. A tireless advocate for her pet social causes, she also believes in pampering herself and her partner of over a decade.

Direct talkers can be intimidating, a bit rough, highly cognitive, or some of each, but the people who are drawn to them relish those aspects. Direct talkers are clear when they're pleased and will accept nothing less than the best for their lovers and themselves. They know themselves well, mind and body, and take pride in self-enhancement. There may not be much poetry when they talk dirty, but it's smoldering and strong. Many direct talkers can often be found in power couples or with younger partners who appreciate their abilities and leadership in many areas.

Rochelle prefers to be active and savors opportunities to initiate hot kisses without warning, and sometimes more. When she talks dirty she gets to the point by making brazen statements that rock her husband even after all of these years. He still remembers one of their early times together, when he was hesitant to kiss her roughly. She pulled back, fingers in his hair, and nearly growled as she quietly instructed him to open his mouth to her before she resumed the kiss.

There was no threat or anger in her tone. It was an animalistic expression of her sexual need for him, one which he was very happy to oblige. In softer moments, Rochelle will look up from a piece of fruit and explicitly detail how the taste of its flesh reminds her of him, followed by a mischievous smile.

The Naughty Tease

While Rochelle always seems to be on top of things and in control in her relationship, Marny is attracted more to men with those qualities. She takes pride in her appearance and has a gift for recognizing and encouraging the best in those around her. Marny isn't always as confident as she'd like to be, but when she's caught up in the moment at work or in the bedroom she knows just how good she can be.

Some of her boyfriends have been better men than others, but she cherishes something about each one long after the relationship is over. I've never met someone who's so good at staying friends with exes, a quality I admire deeply in her. One of her greatest joys in life is flirting, and she's at her best when she has two, three, or even four men in her life. While many of them would like to be her only man, each of them feels special when they spend time with her.

She loves their attention and knows just how to get it with a quick text or voice message. Marny can burn up a phone line or melt a chat window like no other. She's the quintessential dirty tease, offering scintillating tidbits that entice her lovers into giving her the dirty talk she longs to hear. Marny is most confident when those around her are clearly happy to spend time with her and realize that their lives are better for having her in it. If this happens on a good hair and makeup day, then she's absolutely unstoppable. Her students stay in touch with her for years, and her friendships stretch back to elementary school.

Naughty teases enjoy tempting their partners into taking charge and making sure that they stay on their lovers' minds at all times. They're masterful at adapting to their partners, sometimes a little too much so, but usually with amazing results. These are the ladies with a sly grin whenever a text message sounds on their phones!

While naughty teases adore pleasure and attention as much as any other style of dirty talker, they share the ability to entice action out of their partners with sweet talkers. Both are ready to compliment their lovers, but these teases take an extra naughty turn and feed the fires constantly. Naughty teases are often the ones who carry on long-distance relationships with the most success because of their dedication to consistent (and very sexual) communication.

The choice of wording runs the spectrum from blue to blushing pink with these flirts. While Marny prefers to nurture relationships in which she can be direct, other naughty teases choose to drop hint after hint until their partner takes the bait. This type of dirty talker can seduce her sweetie into telling her exactly how they want to be pleased, in step-by-step detail. While naughtiness is essential to these ladies, the tease is just as important. Marny makes sure that every boyfriend leaves her bed anticipating the next encounter at the same time that he's relishing the last one.

These styles are only a small sample from the many women I've met, but they should help get your creative juices flowing. Now that you've met the sweet talker, the direct talker, and the naughty tease, which parts of each remind you of yourself? Which left you wishing for a description that sounded more like you? Take a few moments and imagine how I'd write about you after spending time with you at your best. Give your thoughts shape by turning to Chapter 12 and filling out the "Dirty Talk Style Guide" worksheet.

Each of these women and styles begins when she nurtures a side of herself that makes her feel confident, deserving, and sensual. When she's in an environment or situation that encourages her sexual power and confidence, dirty talk becomes a natural and easy form of erotic expression. She asks for what she wants, whether she's initiating or enticing her partner to do so.

Although dirty talk styles can vary widely, these elements are always there and consistently successful in producing the kind of romantic encounters that she wants. Coming up with the right words becomes a form of fun and exploration, instead of a stressful scramble. Just as wonderfully, these women's partners prefer their honest sexual selves over any fantasy women they had imagined before.

Key Points

- Discovering your own confident moment can help you understand more about your dirty talking style. Use the exercise in Chapter 12 to explore your moment and reflect on what it tells you about your most comfortable style.
- There are many styles of dirty talk, including the sweet talker, the direct talker, and the naughty tease.
- Break through any stereotypes you have about who talks dirty to create your own style!

EXERCISE

Flip to Chapter 12 and fill out the worksheet to help you "Find Your Confident Moment." Then turn to the "Dirty Talk Style Guide" to begin translating your confident moment into a style of talking dirty that's all your own.

FIVE

Envision Your Character

Cameryn: Well, get down here between my legs. Ah-ah-aah. Stop here. I slide my palm down your cheek, and then run my fingers through your hair to the back of your head and slowly bring you forward to about six or eight inches away from my pussy. I want you to watch, but not taste, just yet. I want you to be desperate. Are you desperate?

Eric: Yes!

Cameryn: No, you're not. You just sit there and watch my right hand while it trails up my inner thigh. I slowly inch my hand up until my index finger is resting just above my clit. I press my finger down and pull up hard, so that my pink lips are stretched up, long and tight. When I release my finger, the lips relax back down into soft velvet folds. You can smell me, warm and musky. Smells good, doesn't it?

Eric: Oh yeah, oh yeah.

When Nicky dances, she introduces her wide-eyed crowds to a side of herself that she only dreamed about a few years ago. Colorful veils, two decorative sabers, tiny candles in palm-sized glass balls, and tubes of body glitter fill her dance kit. Her approach is announced by the music of the metal disks that drip from the breasts and hips of her belly dance ensemble.

"When I dance, I tease and talk nasty to my entire audience. But I do it with my body."

Her lashes flutter demurely, lined in thick, black-liquid eyeliner, as she sips a cup of tea with me between performances at the local Greek restaurant. It's a busy Saturday night, and she knows that the diners are there as much to see her as to savor the hearty phyllo pies and feta potatoes on their plates. Later, she'll slip home to relieve the babysitter and check on her two young sons who will (she hopes) be fast asleep.

By this time Monday, she'll be kicking off her respectable pumps after a long day at the office. But all of that is a world away now. In a few minutes she'll step between the tables to demonstrate her shimmies, camel walk, and stomach undulations to the sound of her own finger cymbals and a saucy track of drum music.

Showing Off Your Facets

Nicky is a different person in the office than in her sons' bedrooms or at the restaurant. Yet all of these people are authentic parts of her dynamic personality.

"I'm not acting any of those places. They're just different parts of who I am, I guess. Don't get me wrong, I didn't spend my childhood longing to shake it for strangers! This is a side of me that I discovered after the boys were born. Sometimes I look at myself in the mirror before I go out and it takes me a minute to recognize my reflection. But, as soon as I do, I know it's my fierce side and I want it to come out and play."

Nicky didn't dance at home while her husband was there until she'd been taking classes for nearly two years; she wasn't ready to share her fierce side until then. Now she says she puts on a private show for him at least once a month, without the body glitter.

"It never comes out of the carpet, and there's enough of it around from after my shows anyway," she laughs.

Like all of us women, Nicky is akin to a finely cut diamond. An uncut diamond is dull and lifeless. It's the addition of facets that makes it gleam with an inner fire. Each side is capable of catching the light in a distinctive way. The difference is subtle but sure. A cut diamond will shine slightly differently depending on the light and how you hold it.

Building on a dirty talk style is like turning a diamond and appreciating how the new side sparkles. Years ago, Nicky realized that she felt most confident when she felt in charge of her body and aware of it. She explains that the isolation exercises (moving one area of the body while holding the others still) in belly dancing drew her to her first class, and the opportunity to wear a jingle belt and look good barefoot kept her coming. As she grew confident during her classes, the dance moves became a natural extension of herself. Her fierce side had waited patiently, but once she discovered that facet of herself it was eager to sparkle and spring to life.

She's wordless for tonight's audience, but Nicky confesses that she's discovered that she likes to talk a bit during her shows for Jon.

"I pull out the slower moves for him, working my stomach and chest muscles and using my hair, doing it more like a lap dance. It gives me a chance to whisper in his ear and kiss him."

What does she say?, I ask.

"Whatever my fierce side wants to say! Sometimes I tell him how turned on I am, or how turned on I'm going to make him . . ." Before she can tell me more, the host signals that he's about to start the next track on her drum CD. She quickly jingles out of the employee's lounge and into the dining area, pausing just long enough to smile at herself in the mirror by the door.

Nicky's confident moments revolve around her mindfulness of her own body and lead to a lusty, full-bodied, and carefully paced seduction style. This style is reflected in her dirty talk; phrases are uttered one by one, each word chosen as much for the sound of its letters as for its meaning.

"The way you watch me makes me so moist. My body lusts for your touch."

Sometimes she simply lists adjectives and adverbs, naming her sensations (and his responses) while she dances, grinds, and teases her husband.

"Soft. Warm. Wet. Hot. Throbbing. Pressing. Wanton. Juicy. Need."

She's developed her facet into a fleshed-out character, grounded solidly in a naturally occurring part of herself. Because it comes from her, she isn't acting when she takes on this part of her character: She's simply highlighting her fierce side as a newly engaged woman holds her diamond in the sun to show it off.

Getting Into Character

Once you have a firm grasp on your dirty talk style, you're ready for the real fun to begin. It's time to bring your style to life by fleshing it out into a functional character—a full side of your personality that's ready to come out and play. Your first character can be as close to your day-to-day self or as wildly imaginative as you like. Between all of your potential styles and the range of characters that each can spawn, there's a limitless number of opportunities to build and flex your dirty talking muscles! Don't let this overwhelm you now, though. The most important thing is for you to have fun getting your feet wet while staying true to what turns you on and makes you feel confident.

If you're home right now, bring your book with you to your bedroom and get ready to explore. You can also close your eyes and envision your bedroom, if you're away from home. Explore your room and touch (or imagine touching) various items that look sensual to the skin. Keep your style in mind and everything you've learned about your confidence while you uncovered your dirty talk style.

Allow yourself to gravitate to items that inspire your confidence. Explore your shoes, jewelry, lingerie, and anything else you might wear, adorn yourself with, or carry as part of an outfit or costume. Continue moving through your room, and other rooms as needed, until you've settled on an item that symbolizes your new dirty talk style and represents your confident moment—whether or not you're wearing it then. This treasure will be the core of your first dirty talk character; place it somewhere special and in plain view.

When I was in high school, my girlfriends and I used to play the underwear game, a giggle-inducing little time waster in which we told each other what our underwear meant about our personalities. There were actually two versions: The first involved interpreting that day's choice, while the other required that we describe our ideal piece of lingerie for the others to interpret. While I wouldn't exactly depend on such a game for my daily horoscope, there was something to be said for the idea. A basic pair of white or flesh-toned bikini briefs signals a more practical mood. On the other hand, racy, lacy French silk knickers are clearly meant to be seen, even if only by the wearer.

We've all heard the experts on women's daytime television extolling the benefits of well-fitted bras and fancy panties to boost our confidence and natural magnetism, along with our sex appeal. It's true, of course. Those French knickers can certainly put some sass in your strut! They remind us of a certain side of ourselves, and they encourage us to think of ourselves erotically.

The item you've just chosen says something just as special, confident, sassy, and encouraging about the way you want to talk dirty to your lovers. Hold it in your hands, close your eyes, and breathe deeply. What's your chosen item telling you about yourself? Imagine that your item could whisper to you if you listened carefully—allow it to tell you more about this budding side of yourself.

How does it want to be worn or held? What does it want to tell others about who you can be, about the kind of vixen that you're preparing to unleash? Is it something that others would expect you to choose, or is it surprising? What sensual words might describe the way this item appeals to every sense? Take a moment to write down your thoughts; you might find it useful to use the "Sensual Item Guide" in Chapter 12.

Once you've finished answering these questions, go back and reread what you've written. This time, allow the item to represent an erotic character stemming from a facet of yourself. Apply each answer to yourself, and use them to describe who you can be as a seductive dirty talker. It may feel strange to think of yourself with all of these positive, attractive, inspiring, and seductive attributes. Do your best not to put yourself down or make excuses about how this activity didn't work for you. Trust me, it did. You're just learning something new about yourself!

When I asked Greta to do this activity, she struggled. First, she had trouble finding something sensual to linger on in her bedroom. She and Laurie had been using the room for spare storage since the baby turned their crafts room into a nursery. We were also working on how their bedroom symbolized their relationship (and how clearing up one could definitely help the other), but that day we were seeking a bridge to some inspired dirty talk. After Greta found her item, she found it difficult to believe that it had anything in common with her own sensual side or that it could inspire her romantic style of dirty talk.

Before Greta found her item, she held up a shoe or two, a necklace, and a pair of comfy athletic socks. I turned them all away, waiting for her face to tell me that she'd found a meaningful treasure. Her eyes finally lit up as she produced a satin clutch she hadn't used in three years. She'd bought it for her union ceremony with Laurie, back before either of them went by "Mommy."

After their honeymoon, the clutch took up residence in a corner of the closet, never again to see the light of day or the neon of night. She held it up, and the rich black satin reflected the light with a deep gleam, giving the ruched surface an enticing sense of visual texture. It brought out the olive tone of her skin beautifully, the delicate beadwork at the edge drawing the eye to the healthy pink of her fingernails. It was a lush fabric that wanted to be touched.

This was not the kind of clutch that's forgotten on a table or left behind in the women's room. A smile crossed Greta's lips and her hand smoothed over the clutch, remembering the special afternoon, her in a feminine black satin skirt suit, Laurie in a smoldering red gown. I asked Greta to tell me about the clutch, how she picked it over other handbags, and how it made her feel when she carried it after their ceremony. I also urged her to describe how it appealed to her senses in vivid detail, mixing adjectives with memories. As she spoke, I took notes of her exact words, so we'd have them ready when it was time to use them to describe and inspire her.

Shortly after the ceremony, Laurie got a big promotion and Greta started her own home business. Then they began the long, stressful two-year process of adopting little Adrian. He'd been with them for six months now, and they felt it was time to bring their family back into balance. While Adrian certainly deserved limitless attention (and received it), they also wanted to relearn how to prioritize their relationship, to be partners, friends, and lovers for each other again.

As with many home-based professionals, Greta's work wardrobe had shifted to sweatpants and T-shirts, mixed with the occasional meeting or conference suit. Makeup was rare now, and her long hair was often swept up in a clip. When Laurie wanted to relax after a hard day of work, Greta already had cabin fever from being in the house all day. To top it off, it felt like Greta sometimes went days without a meaningful adult conversation. While Adrian was a well-behaved darling, he just wasn't able to hold up his end of a discussion on Greta's most annoying client or favorite book.

It's not surprising that Greta felt nothing like the satin clutch in her hand, but she wished she could. She could even remember identifying with some of the words she chose, but not in a long time.

From her list of words, phrases, and memories that described the satin handbag, Greta was able to pick one word that she felt might sometimes describe her in the present: accomplished. I asked her what she meant by that word. After all, I have an image of "accomplished" in my head, but it was important to know how she envisioned the word. She talked a bit about her graduate education, her publications, and her hard-earned success as a new entrepreneur. Eventually she talked more about how being accomplished felt and what sorts of things inspired it in her.

As she shared more and more, I began to draw connections between her thoughts on accomplished and other words on her list. It was easy to move to important, then treasured and valuable. When she felt that way she also felt powerful, organized, and worth holding onto. From there, it wasn't a far stretch to identify with long-lost feelings like touchable, sensual, and eye-catching. As each word took root in her self-concept, she began to smile, unconsciously holding the black, shiny treasure to her chest with excitement.

Whether or not she felt that way frequently, she had to admit that every word on her list was a side of herself that she could call forth if the time and place were just right. Many of them were words she also wanted to weave into her dirty talk. For Greta, complimenting Laurie's body and making her sweetie feel prized were important aspects of seduction. When she made Laurie feel erotically treasured, Greta felt even more important and turned on, too.

Recognizing Your Sensual Confidence

As you ponder your own treasure, whatever it is, take the time to write your thoughts, feelings, and associations. If you have mixed feelings about the item, focus on the positive aspects or choose another. Like Greta, you may initially feel like none of those delightful descriptors apply to you, at least not at this time in your life. Begin with the term closest to accurate now, or at least every now and then. Explore it, as Greta explored the word *accomplished*, and expand on it until you begin to see links between your starter words and the words around it.

I encourage you to pull out your "Confident Moment" worksheet for comparison. This can help you identify bridges from your treasure to you at your best, most confident moments. Indeed, each activity in this book is designed to tie into the next so that if you get stuck at any point you can refer to your previous work and find personalized inspiration in your very own words!

Greta found an authentic dirty talk character by combining her confident moment, dirty talk style, and sensual treasure. That moment stemmed from the experience of presenting her business plan to potential funders and coming back with the financial support she needed to launch her company. She made her funders feel like a part of something special: Her vision for an innovative product that would help others. Her strong, enticing, and confident presence combined with her ability to verbalize her passionate feelings about the topic.

Greta felt that this was a natural match for a romantic, strong, dirty talking style that took the lead in making her partner know how attractive she was to Greta. She rejected the label of seductress, and instead called her style "irresistible love." Greta didn't even like to say "dirty talk," instead opting for "sweet talk." Talk about a departure from stereotypes about who talks dirty and how!

Greta realized from her sensual treasure, the black satin clutch, that she also wanted to bring a sense of class and elegance to her sweet-talking activities. And she wanted to bring a sense of showing off to the experience, even if no one else was actually there to witness them. Sensual language would also be important, as she wanted her words to sound as smooth as satin, yet with a bit of sparkle and texture. We decided that she'd think over our notes for a week, and work up a script that felt natural for herself in that kind of scenario. Meanwhile, when she found a phrase that really felt right, she would send it to Laurie as a text message, just for fun!

The memories, personality attributes, and special sensual objects in our lives hold a great deal of meaning. They can tell us about who we are when we're at our best, who we long to become, and what's most important to us as erotic beings, whether we're single, dating openly, or in a relationship. When we take ourselves and our sexuality for granted, it's easy to ignore or discount these sources of inspiration, just like we ignore our own sensuality and desires.

Our erotic sensuality, the source of our best dirty talk inspiration, can sometimes become a quiet whisper. By paying close attention to the meanings behind these memories and objects, we can focus in on the whisper and hear what it's telling us. Eventually, it'll become louder and clearer, until we find our own brand of sweet talk spilling from our lips naturally, easily, and oh so seductively!

Key Points

- Your dirty talk style can lead to the creation of many characters or sides of yourself that set the mood and create inspiration for your erotic words.
- Discovering a sensual item and considering what it represents about how you feel the most sexually empowered can help you develop a more authentic character that truly represents a facet of yourself.
- Dirty talk characters should be an honest representation of one part of our sexual energy, not a creation designed just to please our partners. Being turned on and aware of your erotic side will turn both of you on more than any false pretense.

EXERCISE

Use the "Sensual Item Guide" in Chapter 12. Combined with your dirty talk style, this can help you develop your first seductive character for getting in the right mood to share your naughty thoughts.

SIX

Practice Your Seductive Style

Cameryn: I'm gonna reach my finger down further and trace my labia, up one side and down the other, just running my fingertip along the edges and tugging slightly so you can see the darker inner folds, slick with my juice. You're getting thirsty now too, aren't you?

Eric: Yesss . . .

Cameryn: You wanna taste it?

Eric: Yeah, oh, yeah.

Cameryn: I'm gonna dip my fingers in my pussy, two fingers, and draw them out, sticky wet. Tilt your head back and open your mouth, baby.

Eric: Mmmmm . . .

With your confidence high, your style and character in mind (thanks to inspiration from your sensual treasure), the only thing between you and a hot night of dirty talk is a bit of practice! Seductive words will be slipping from your lips with ease and confidence, but not until you've had a bit of practice getting into character and enjoying this naughtier side of yourself. Body posture and the choice of authentic language can do a great deal to help you feel natural, so you can lose yourself in the moment without accidentally going silent.

And now that we've learned how to begin, it's just as important to consider where to stop and when to back off to a safer or simpler place. After all, this is the art of dirty talk, not a major theater performance! You certainly don't want to miss out on your own pleasure just for the sake of a good show. Keeping everything in balance is an art in itself; thankfully, it's also easy to practice.

But what about vocabulary building? How can you practice without a list of naughty words tucked into your memory (or at least your iPhone)? Unlike some magazine articles and other dirty talk guides out there, we've been exploring dirty talk from the perspective of your pleasure and joy. All of this must stem from your authentic self to avoid a performance that fools your sweetie (for now) into thinking you're turned on yet leaves your libido in the cold. That means that I want you to get your feet under yourself for a bit before we start making lists of sweet somethings together.

Back in my undergraduate days, I had a professor who repeated a bit of classic research with every class. First, she asked half of the class to step out. Then she directed the remaining students to make a quick sketch of a cat. After we'd submitted our scribbling, she instructed us to put our heads down and remain silent. She then had the other students return to the room and asked them to do the same task. But this time she provided an illustration on the board of a speedily drawn outline of a sitting cat with cartoon eyes and long whiskers.

Although she hadn't done anything to lead students in the second half to believe that they should follow her example, that stack was mostly composed of round-bottomed, cartoony, sitting cats with busy whiskers. The first group, however, had a variety of cats in all positions and styles from stick figures to semirealistic pencil renderings of cats lounging or playing. A few creative types even had a cat from the back, tail high and rear exposed. The first group included some peripherals, as well, like little fish or meows in the corners. The latter group contained no such creativity.

Even when we're encouraged to be creative, we still have a natural, human tendency to follow the examples of others. Sometimes this ends in a better result, but it also stifles our creative potential. This is why I'm teaching dirty talk practice before vocabulary. I want to make sure that your creative juices are flowing before you hear what others are saying. That way, their examples can serve as tools instead of templates.

Sexy Homework

Practicing your dirty talk should be an exciting, heart-fluttering task from the start. If you find yourself becoming uncomfortably nervous or concentrating too hard, take a moment to stop and reconnect with your inner desires. Remember, this is all about the honest outpouring of your own lusty urges and thoughts. Overactive nerves and a churning mind are almost always a sure sign that you're focusing on your performance over your pleasure. Although it seems counterintuitive, you'll do much better if you relax and bumble forward without pressure than if you try to preplan each moment in pursuit of the perfect phrases.

Clumsy words that offer an honest expression of your inner heat are a far greater turn-on then a faked performance, and they'll feel better to you. As in all matters of the bedroom, ladies, faking may seem worth it at the time, but it only cheats you out of your pleasure in the long run and gives you another set of lies to keep straight. Anxiety and hard concentration can also be a sign that you're not yet sure of what you want or how to put it in words. In addition to continuing your private exploration with your body and your fantasies, you may also find that letting yourself relax and say whatever comes to mind may actually help you discover a bit more about yourself!

Where's the best place to start? Why, with yourself! Remember your first pair of fancy high heels? You quickly realized how important it was to wear them around the house before striking out to conquer your next formal event. It felt odd to pack lunches, do the laundry, and curl up in the corner with your favorite book while wearing a pair of high-fashion pumps.

But when you were towering high while navigating your way through the crowd to the bar, you realized just how important it was to practice by dodging the cat on the way to the refrigerator earlier in the week. It's just as important to practice your dirty talk amid your regular chores and tasks. Get your wobbles out on your own, and you'll be ready to impress your sweetie when the moment arrives (and you'll be better at catching yourself if you do stumble).

So the absolute best place to begin practicing your dirty talk is during your most private moments, while you're alone. Whether you call it personal time, self-care, or simply masturbating, it's the perfect time and place to practice. I could suggest you parade all over your house trying to talk dirty, but until you've done it in the pleasure of self-intimacy and exploration, it won't have quite the right ring to it.

Not only is self-pleasure linked to a wide variety of healthy individual and relationship outcomes by a long list of research studies, it's a handy time (no pun intended) to try out new sexual scenarios without the pressure of an audience. If you don't yet masturbate regularly and comfortably, or it has never done much for you, I strongly encourage you to visit my Web site, or even to contact me directly. I suspect that you're only a bit of support and a few suggestions away from understanding what all the fuss is about, even if you feel far from it. I've helped many women learn to masturbate long after they've had sex, tied the knot (once, twice, or more), had children and given up on the idea of self-stimulation, and I'm not the only professional doing this important work. No matter what, everyone deserves the pleasure of self-stimulation and orgasm, regardless of any negative past efforts or experiences.

If you fancy yourself a silent masturbator, allow yourself to open up with guttural sounds and sighs at first. Many of us learned to masturbate in unfortunate situations that forced us to be quiet, speedy, and very still. I'm constantly meeting women who are goal oriented when they masturbate, too. For them, it's how they fall asleep at night, keep the headaches at bay, or get a little relief from menstrual cramps.

Whether you're a sneaky masturbator or you only let your fingers do the walking to get it out of the way, it's time to relax and enjoy! Give yourself permission to luxuriate and explore. You can lounge in the tub with scented candles if you like, but I personally recommend surrounding yourself with a good bottle of lube and a high-quality sex toy instead.

Lubricant can help us relax, become aroused by a wet touch, and touch ourselves with more pleasure and less overstimulation. A good vibrator offers intense, tireless stimulation so that we can lie back and enjoy the ride more easily. Visit the resources page on my website at exploringintimacy.com to read my suggestions for choosing a lubricant and a sex toy, if you don't already have these items or are unsure whether you've chosen products made from healthy ingredients. These are some of my most popular workshop handouts.

Releasing Your Moan

Back to those sighs and moans I was talking about! As you begin to stretch out and get yourself in the mood with a few delicious fantasies, your lube, and your toy, be mindful of your relaxation and breath. You should have plenty of time to yourself for this exercise, not to mention privacy. And turn off your cell phone! Turn it all the way off and leave it in the other room, don't just put it on vibrate; your toy doesn't appreciate the competition, anyway.

With no distractions and plenty of time to enjoy yourself, take your time to touch yourself in the ways you wish your partners would. You know what I'm talking about: gentle yet firm and without any hint of rush. The best partner's only agenda is enjoying your pleasure, and you should be your own very best lover.

As you remind yourself what it means to be cherished and pampered, allow yourself to breathe in deeply through your nose, filling your lungs and pausing for a moment. Then open your mouth and exhale in a luxuriating sigh that releases your stress and brings your focus to the sensations throughout your body. Notice the feeling of your soft bed sheets (or couch, or wherever you may be), feel your weight pressing into your bed, and notice how some areas of your skin are warmer or smoother than others.

Release yourself from any judgment or stressful thoughts by acknowledging negative feelings and asking them to continue on their way, should they happen at all. Let each exhalation be an expression of your relaxation and pleasure. Whether you sound sleepy, grunty, loud, shy, giggly, gritty, animalistic, or like an opera singer, your sounds are absolutely perfect just the way they are. Allow yourself to experiment until you find sounds that turn you on to utter, as well as to hear. If you've ever heard a woman in ecstasy in a porn movie, or even in a mainstream flick, you may find yourself sounding like that at first until you find what works for you. Remember the example of the cat drawing; this may or may not be the way your body feels hottest expressing itself.

Although we have fixed ideas of how a woman in pleasure should sound, nothing is hotter than an authentic expression of your erotic sensations, no matter how it comes out! Your noises will progress as you pleasure yourself more and more, culminating in a very vocal orgasm. There's no need to stop at only one if you're enjoying yourself, of course!

If you find yourself falling quiet at any point, refocus on your breathing and begin with deep exhalations until you feel that your sounds are representing your pleasure once again. It's completely normal for it to take weeks before this begins to come naturally. This is wonderful news, because practicing is fun and also healthy for your body!

Useful Fantasies

Many women have told me that they concentrate on an intense fantasy or they simply try to empty their minds and reach for their orgasm to get the deed done. These women often fall quiet because they're disconnected from their bodies. Instead of breathing, moaning, and feeling pleasure, they're gritting their teeth, scrunching their brows, holding their breaths, and concentrating far too hard.

I'm a strong proponent of fantasies, but sometimes they can blind us to permitting ourselves to explore and feel pleasure throughout our bodies and those of our partners. All good things are best in balance! If you find yourself avoiding any thoughts about what's happening in the moment, allow yourself to consider why this may be and what might help you return to your body and your sensuality.

Sometimes all it takes is an effort to mix things up a bit and raise our self-pleasure to a more intense level of revelry. Other times, it's a warning flag for a personal or relational issue that's gone ignored for too long. It's worth taking the time to resolve these issues, as they often pop up at the worst times. Again, allow your mind to return to your body, and play with your breath and noises until they find ways to naturally express your pleasure.

Once you've established this baseline, you can return to your fantasies and begin to add them again, while keeping them in balance with your connection to the moment. If you enjoy the thought of your lover caressing your thighs, for example, don't just think about it: Do it! Allow the movements of your hands (and toys), and the responses of your body, to connect with your fantasies and enhance them.

Dreaming of having your hands sensually pinned? Reach up to your headboard or tuck one hand beneath your pillow. Ready to place your fantasy lover's hand on your body and show them how to touch you? Enjoy the opportunity to emulate the experience for yourself. And what's your dream lover saying to you? What sounds are they making and drawing from your lips? Answer your partner out loud, whether in a whisper or a roar. You may even enjoy giving voice to their dirty talk along with responding to it.

There are no rules or limits. Enjoy the opportunity to experiment and find what you like. No one is there to see you, so there's no need to feel shy or silly. Even if someone were there to watch, I'm convinced that whatever makes a woman feel sexy also makes her look sexy.

Stoking Your Sexual Energy

What a vision of lust and eroticism you are at this point! Your body language is in sync with your fantasies and driving them forward, and your breathing and vocalizations convey your pleasure and satisfaction. Who knew you had this kind of sexual connection at your fingertips (quite literally) besides you and I? Thus inspired, you're ready to let your sensual energy flow out into your daily life.

There's no need to lock these expressions of your authentic pleasure in the nightstand with your toys and lube! Let them flow into the kitchen. Allow each bite of fruit salad to linger in your mouth, drawing contented sighs as you allow the sweet juices to seduce your tongue.

Are you enjoying your burger? Moan to it softly, and smile as a dab of ketchup finds your lip for you to lick off. Do whatever it takes to enjoy your meal, even if that means leaving the silverware in the drawer so you can feel the food as you feed yourself with your fingers. Be sure to provoke jealous glances with every nibble of chocolate.

Don't stop at the kitchen. Next time you slide on your stockings, take your time smoothing them over your legs and appreciating the sensations with a soft breath and perhaps a compliment to yourself. I shouldn't even need to tell you that morning showers now deserve a few extra minutes of enjoyment.

As women we have hours and hours of personal upkeep and beautifying rituals every week (or every day, for some of us). At one point they may have been fun and sensual, but eventually they became habits. You can bring sensuality to many of these tasks by being mindful and aware of your body at all times, and taking delight in interacting with it.

It can be fun and flirty to share these activities with your partner, and tempting to use their feedback to adjust your approach. Resist the urge to switch from authentic enjoyment to an erotic performance! There are many wonderful times and places for erotic performances, but this isn't one of them. This is your opportunity to authentically and honestly explore your own sensations of pleasure, and then vocalize them.

I hope that each of you will be surrounded by partners who find your uninhibited pleasure arousing and completely perfect. If yours does not, I encourage you to consider whether this is a sign of a larger problem in the relationship. Ask for their loving support, and ask them to do whatever work is necessary on their end for them to be able to respect and adore your arousal. There's no wrong way to sound, move, smell, taste, or feel when you're in pleasure. Simply immerse yourself in what comes naturally and enjoy your body.

Now that you've practiced expanding and playing with your authentic sexual and sensual pleasure, you're ready to learn how to incorporate props and vocabulary-building activities. You've established a sound foundation in your body, your fantasies, and your eroticism. Adding props and expanding your language can now become a way to grow even more into your sexual energy, and bring your lover along with you for every delightful moment.

Key Points

- Self-pleasure is a fun (and essential) way to learn about your sexuality and begin to practice your dirty talk. Start with moans, sighs, cries, and any other noise that could come naturally if you let yourself be loud.
- Once you're able to vocalize, begin to verbalize by touching yourself while you fantasize and adding any words that fit with the moment.
- You can use this technique as a bold way to seduce your lovers by showing them what you've learned and how much you enjoy a little time with yourself.

EXERCISE

Are you a confident, accomplished woman when it comes to self-stimulation, or do you find yourself rushed, shy, or unsure? Give yourself time and permission to explore your body. Your ultimate goal is to find three different ways that you like to orgasm by yourself, but don't rush yourself! Enjoy the journey of exploration and take as long as you need. If you're unsure about how to do this, turn to the resources in Chapter 14. You can also visit my online resource guides on lube, vibrators, and more at exploringintimacy.com/library/resources.

SEVEN

Create the Perfect Words

Cameryn: That's right. You're going to suck it all clean, between my fingers, the edges of my nails. Tastes so good, doesn't it?

Eric: Mmm HMMMM.

Cameryn: You want some more?

Eric: Yeah, yeah, please, yeah.

Cameryn: Please what?

Eric: Please can I eat your pussy?

You have your style and character, perhaps more than one, and you've practiced. Your moans, sighs, and growls are beginning to make the neighbors wonder who's snuck into your room when they weren't looking. Your sweeties are eagerly listening at the door and wondering when they get to join the fun.

Now it's time to start putting together words and scripts. Over this chapter and the next three, you'll begin with a mindful focus on the senses, progressing to the three levels of increasingly naughty dirty talk, and finally you'll add your fantasies. By the time we're done, you'll be at no loss for words!

Finding Inspiration

Surrounding ourselves with inspiration, from our own masturbation experiences to accessories that tap into our confident selves, can help build the mood and our confidence while inspiring naughty utterances. Now that we've built a firm foundation in our authentic eroticism and pleasure, it's time to build our vocabulary, explore the use of naughty props, and learn how to complement the perfect situation with the hottest words! With a little practice, you can even train your sweetie to invoke the same excitement by asking them questions that'll bring out the dirty talker in them, too. But first, let's learn how to draw inspiration from the experts of dirty talk and fantasy through sexy movies, books, and other media.

Sexy books are one of my favorite suggestions for couples and singles looking for dirty talk inspiration and sample words or scripts. The market is flooded with all kinds of naughty reading material, from heart-pounding novels in every setting imaginable to compilations of themed stories written by various authors. You can even find free material on the Web, although I prefer to support local authors, and I also find that mainstream books are of far better quality than most online offerings. Whatever your tastes, there's likely to be a book filled with inspiration just waiting for you.

"I admit it," Astra began, "I'm not a big fan of most porn, but I sure do like dirty stories. Or 'romance novels,' as my mom calls them. Call it weird, but we even swap our favorite books. I'm not sure why I can trade my flowery brand of smut with my mother but not my girlfriend."

Astra even shared that they both dog-ear their favorite pages so that she and her mother can linger over particularly juicy bits of their favorite softcover reads. Despite sharing books with her mother every month since Astra started her MBA and turned to romance novels for an erotic escape, she had never offered one to any of her partners over the years. Her boyfriends had laughed off her habit as a silly, girlish pastime, and her current partner, Chrystal, had no idea what she hid in her gym bag to help pass the time on the stepper.

"Why not pass her a copy of one you're done with, maybe a really good one?" I asked.

"I'm just too shy. I mean, look at these things! They're not exactly great pieces of literature."

"Who cares? I bet parts of them still turn you on, don't they?"

She nodded, a slight blush coloring her cheeks.

"There is this one crazy book I've kept for years about a woman who runs an avocado farm, of all things . . ." she said, as she began to recite her favorite parts from memory.

The Gift of Vulnerability

Astra hits on two important points, without even knowing it. The first is that we might be the most shy around the very same people with whom we assume we should be sharing our favorite fantasies and sweet somethings. Astra's mother represents unconditional, nonsexual support and caring. Astra's girlfriend, as sweet as she is, leaves Astra feeling much more emotionally vulnerable. If her mother laughs at the scene under the thick shade of the avocado trees, it's not a personal insult. But if Chrystal laughs, it's another story.

We worry about our lover's opinions of us on a far deeper level, especially their opinions of our sexual selves. While Astra is confident that Chrystal would still respect her in the morning after reading one of her romance books, that doesn't help ease her embarrassment worry. Whether we're sharing fantasies or erotica stories that turned us on, or narrating our own arousal for our partners as we touch ourselves, our loins (to borrow a term from the avocado book) are not nearly as vulnerable as our hearts.

When we share our dirty thoughts and swap naughty inspiration, we're giving a gift to our lovers that's as fragile as it is valuable. Before you begin, I suggest that you sit down with your sweetheart and let them know that you want to share something special about who you are as a sexual person. Remember that sharing your interests is not an obligation for your partner to like it or want to include it in their sex life with you.

Whether or not you and your partner's interests turn out to be the same, your trust and confidence is still a gift, and it should be received as such. Be sure to let them know as much and get ready to receive the gift of their own dirty dreams and notions when you're done. Let them know how you want them to respond and how they can make you feel comfortable and cherished during the conversation. And remember, not every fantasy or dirty talk inspiration is best shared! While Astra did decide to share her avocado adventures, we first discussed whether she wanted to keep that story as a private inspiration or make it a shared source of naughty insight.

Although Chrystal admitted that she wasn't a big fan of romance novels, she was deeply touched by Astra's trust. Within a week, Astra came home to find a picnic spread in the sunroom, complete with sliced avocado as finger food and chilled sangria. Chrystal had even worn a tie to use as a blindfold on Astra while she described her lips and tongue, just like in the book but better.

Make the Words Yours

It isn't enough to read your book and set it aside. Pick up your highlighter and mark the words, contexts, and descriptions that catch your attention. If a piece of dialogue would be perfect, except for that one word that catches in your throat, use a pen to cross it out and replace it with a better term. Remember, just because you use a word socially or your partner gets the hots for a particular noun, verb, or descriptor doesn't mean you find it sexy.

It can be particularly challenging to think of words for body parts that turn us on. Don't be afraid to explore direct as well as symbolic language in your quest for replacement words, and don't stop until you've shaped your highlighted sections into your perfect dirty talk samples. If you find yourself at a loss, the Internet offers many creative lists of synonyms for anatomy and all the lovely (and nasty) things we can do with it. Cut-and-paste your favorites into your own list and try saying them out loud to make sure you like them as much as you think you will.

Remember to take context into account. At a workshop organized by Amy Jo Goddard, a fantastic sex educator, we were all taking turns reading dirty story snippets. The woman seated across from me donned an English accent, drawing a chorus of giggles from the room, and proceeded to read her script.

At one point she referred to her anus as a "rose bud," delicately making eye contact while letting the phrase slip off her tongue languidly. I had never considered rose bud a sexy term until I heard her say it within that fantasy context, and I've been fond of it ever since. Try saying different words in various tones and imagining how they might be hot. Some won't be hot under any circumstances, and others might surprise you.

Once you've perfected your highlighted bits and pieces, take a deep breath and hand the book over to your sweetie along with a different color of highlighter. Ask them to mark their own favorite parts while they scope out your favorites. Remember that it's OK to have different tastes.

The most important thing is to open your communication about dirty talk and begin to learn what you both might like to hear and say. Although you may be nervous at first, this should be a fun and giggly way for the two of you to share and grow as a couple. Once you know a bit more about what you each like to hear (and say), it'll be hard to resist slipping a naughty phrase or two into your private conversations!

Astra prefers romance novels over other types of literature—porn movies, music lyrics, and other forms of erotic inspiration—but that doesn't mean that you need to limit yourself the same way. I know a particularly daring friend who enjoys rough role-play with her partners. She's fond of quoting a certain CGI-enhanced numerical blockbuster to her lover, pledging that their interlude would not be over quickly. And as popular music becomes increasingly explicit, it provides better and better examples to inspire us (or stick with a classic, which still packs a punch).

Low-Risk Flirting

In the beginning, try out your new phrases and words in low-risk situations: Think of it as a drive-by flirting. Pick up your book, lyrics, or movie quotes and send out a saucy little text message. If you want to take it slower, simply let your lover know that you were flipping through the pages of highlighted sections and thinking of them, without quoting the book at all. Don't forget to make it personal! There's nothing like a simple "and I was thinking of you" at the beginning or end of a note to turn it from subtle and factual to hot and steamy. We'll talk more about the power of this phrase in the next chapter, as I walk you through more detailed exercises on sensual language-building.

Drive-by flirting is a low-risk, yet no less sensual, way to get your naughty messages across. There's no need for your partner to come up with a prompt response, and you can walk away if you'd rather not come up with a follow-up comment right then. Text messages are one of my favorite forms of dirty talk, but e-mails, voice-mail messages, and even notes packed into lunch bags can work just as well.

Imagine your sweetie's face when they open their phone to discover that you just slid your panties off . . . and you're thinking of the look on their face! You might just find out that they've left work a few minutes early to see for themself. Another great time for a drive-by is during house chores, or just before stepping out of the car for a public event. Lean in and whisper the perfect phrase right before you open the door or step off the train together, ensuring that they have plenty to think about while you're out for the evening.

"I love little league games for flirting," blurted out LaQuisha during a workshop in Georgia:

> *All of the parents are leaning in to discuss how their children are doing out on the field. They're grinning, cheering, sharing picnic dinners, and generally having a good old time. To be honest, I just find the games so boring, but I didn't want to be the only one reading a book between my kids' times at bat. So, I decided to see exactly how much I could get away with. My David is a shy man, but he loves discreet attention. Now I spend the game leaning over to whisper about his body, what it does to my body, and how much I'm looking forward to putting a movie on for the kids and disappearing for a few minutes after the game. Those innings practically fly by these days! David looks forward to it, too. He is still too shy to whisper back at the game, but he has started bringing up my dirty talk when we're alone later, so I know he loves it.*

"Yard work. I do it when he is outside working on the yard," replied Sherry:

Marquise takes the car and the yard very seriously, and I appreciate it. I'll usually go out a couple of times to check on him and bring out some iced tea. Every now and then I leave him with a glass as a well as a little hint. Usually I tell him how sexy he looks, all hot and sweaty like that. It's true! I might not be in the mood when he is done, or the kids might be too crazy to sneak upstairs, but at least we're keeping the sexual energy alive somehow. You have to do what you can, especially when you have kids, you know?

Quick Saves

After workshops I always linger for a bit, to let the shyer participants have a chance to ask questions one-on-one. Amy approached me after one, pretending to look at the books next to me before finally gathering the courage to ask a question.

"This is my second time at this workshop. I came yesterday, too, but it's really hard for me to talk like this, and I needed to hear it again. I think I can do something easy, maybe, but I'm so afraid of looking stupid. What if I lose my words, and I'm just standing there in front of him trying to think of something to say? It's so terrifying!" Amy's question is something that a lot of women worry about, and, thankfully, it's something we can work with. Shy ladies, two backup plans are within easy reach: compliments and props.

Your partner turns to find you standing, jaw slightly open but without a single word coming out. You had the perfect thing to say a moment ago, but now it's gone or the situation isn't quite as good as you thought it would be. Your graceful save is as easy as a brief, authentic compliment. Romeo and Cyrano weren't the only ones with a gift for seductive flattery. Some of the best compliments come from the lips of women.

With or without dirty talk, your partner deserves a few honest compliments. When all else fails, tell them what you really think of them at their best!

I had something to say, but all of a sudden I forgot. Looking at your beautiful body does that to me sometimes, sorry.

Sorry, was I staring? You just looked so good right then.

Remember that first date we went on, and how cute you were? Yeah, I was thinking about that.

I know you always do the [insert chore or task here], but sometimes it just hits me how hard you work. You mean the world to me.

If your sweetie insists on an explanation for sudden demonstrative comments, you can always blame me: "Oh, I've been reading another one of those relationship books, and the author reminded me to tell you when I appreciate you. You don't mind, do you?"

Illustrate Your Point

My other suggestion is props. Compliments are the perfect plan B for a drive-by flirting that runs out of gas. But what about when you're in a passionate moment and your reservoir of dirty talk has run dry? You've got your delicious moans and sighs (remember practicing by yourself?), but maybe it's not the right moment for that, either. Now is the time to have a prop handy! A sexy prop can be a lady's best friend in any situation. Pull out your favorite sexy accessory or vibrator and let it do the talking while you wait for inspiration.

When I offer fantasy workshops I often speak about the importance of a good, basic prop to give you confidence and also to buy you time while you pick out your next words. I usually choose one of those long, plastic stems with a soft tuft of thin, rubber strands for a playful little whip. You know the kind—they look just like the popular cat toys with a poof of feathers on one end and the same rubber tassels on the other. This is a perfect prop for dirty talkers, with its tactile quality and a long whippy stem in the middle with which to fiddle.

I pluck one of these lovelies from its vase and begin to tap the rubber tassels in one hand while slowly approaching a lucky audience member who's given me permission to flirt with her. As the toy beats a slow, steady rhythm in my hand, I pause before her and look her boldly in the eye. My fingers run the length of the stem, and then I resume my tapping while I pace a slow circle around her chair. Finally, I stop behind her and place my hand on her shoulder.

"I know what you've been up to. You've been having naughty thoughts during my workshop, haven't you?"

Inevitably she blushes and nods while the rest of the group whistles and watches eagerly. Quietly I walk in front of her, resting the stem on her other shoulder with the feathers lightly brushing the side of her neck.

"I think you like being naughty, though. I think that's why you're here. And you want to be even naughtier when you get home, don't you?"

Three statements and two questions have just occurred, that's all. It took several minutes for the entire exchange, and no matter whom she came with or plans to go home with later, she's already under my spell. In between each statement I had ample time to concentrate on what to say next. I then repeat the example, giving my inner monologue.

"Oh drat, I have no idea what to say. What am I going to do with this toy, anyway? I'll stand here and tap it for a while, so she thinks I'm devious. Still nothing. OK, time to walk behind her. I know! I'll tell her she's been doing something naughty, that always works! With any luck, she'll play along." It's not nearly as sexy when my inner thoughts come out, but it's a solid example of how much a good prop can do for a nervous dirty talker.

You have no sexy, whippy cat toy of your own, you say? Fair enough. But I know you have a vibrator from your homework from the previous chapter (if not, hurry and get one before I notice that you don't have it yet), and that will do just as well. Believe it or not, men like vibrators just as much as women do, so gender is no excuse here. A basic, cylindrical vibe made out of hard plastic, glass, ceramic, or smooth silicone makes a fantastic massage tool. Simply press it between your spread open hands and their back, then lean against it as you roll it up and down their torso.

Male or female, most people enjoy the feeling of a lubricated sex toy on their genitals and anus, too. Just remember not to insert it anally unless it's designed for that (and has a widely flared base to keep it from slipping inside) and you have plenty of high-quality lube, and never move a toy from a vagina to an anus without putting a new condom on it. As you work your sex toy magic, take the opportunity to use some of the words and phrases that you discovered together from those dirty books and movies.

And just like that, your dirty words are dripping from your lips like honey. Thanks to the seductive use of your prop, your body language is quickly falling in line with your new aural seduction techniques. Although imitation may be the highest form of flattery, you can't stop now! It's time to personalize your dirty talk even more, beginning with the senses. Get ready, because you're about to learn how to entice your lover with a fruit salad, of all things.

Key Points

- Learning from the experts is a wonderful way to increase your vocabulary.
- Creative use of a simple, sensual prop can give you inspiration and also buy you time while you concoct your next sexy line.
- Honest, sensual compliments are a fantastic way to practice dirty talk without the pressure of navigating an entire naughty conversation or story.

EXERCISE

Purchase a book or magazine with short erotic stories on a theme that interests you, as well as two highlighters of different colors. Use one highlighter to mark any words, phrases, or sections that catch your eye and turn you on. Feel free to scratch out specific words and replace them with personal favorites to make sections hotter for you. Pass the book and the other highlighter to your lover, and ask them to do the same. When you're done, cuddle up and read your favorite passages to each other.

EIGHT

Linger on the Senses

Cameryn: I have to check something first. I'm going to lean forward and squeeze that cock. Ooh, that's really hard. You're just about ready to pop, huh?

Eric: Yessss! Oh my god, oh my god, oh my god.

Cameryn: Here, I'm going to slide my hips back down to the edge of the chair, my knees flung wide and my pussy spread open, and then pull your head forward. Get in there, baby. Show me how hungry you are. Oh, yeah, nibble and kiss up and down each side, and then bring your lips together right over my clit and give that a nice hard suck.

Eric: Come in my mouth, come in my mouth, please!

Recently, I stood in front of a packed room of sexually adventurous, kinky singles, couples, and groups at a rather adult convention featuring daytime educational classes and debauchery-filled nights. The workshop's topic was fellatio: a seemingly basic skill for such a wild group. Heads nodded and pencils scribbled quickly as attendees took notes on creative techniques, but it wasn't until I began to discuss the importance of sensuality and appreciation that attendees began to cheer their agreement.

I've seen a lot of interesting sexual phenomena during my career, yet this group of people was so saucy and experienced that they made me look like a wide-eyed virgin on prom night. But even sexually savvy folks like those in my audience need a reminder to slow down and bring it back to the sensual basics. Whether you love to recline in leather and platform heels or prefer to spend your evenings in yoga pants, we all need to increase our mindfulness of the foundation of sexual pleasure: our senses. Like every other erotic art, dirty talk starts with sound, smell, taste, sight, and touch.

Learning from the experts is an easy way to gain both vocabulary and a better idea of what you like by hearing from others in a low-pressure atmosphere. After diversifying your vocabulary from carefully evaluated dirty stories, movies, songs, and more, it's time to bring in more of your own favorite words. Yes, you already have a cornucopia of delicious words at your disposal; you've just never thought of using them before. It's easy to become intimidated by the idea of dirty talk and immediately fall back into stereotypes, even when we know better. Just like my kinky workshop audience, it can be deeply inspirational and intimate to immerse ourselves and our partners in a more foundational sensuality.

Flaunting Your Sensuality with Pride

Not only is sensual language deeply erotic, it allows us to personalize dirty talk. Anyone can declare, "I want your hot body so bad. Take your big, strong _____ and put it/them on/in my _____! Oh yes! More!" Other than communicating arousal and giving vague sexual directions, statements like this can be exchanged between any individuals in an erotic context. It can be very hot to hear or say such blunt, dirty things, but in the end you'll be no closer to your partner than you were before. Sensual language makes our partners and ourselves emotionally vulnerable in ways that not only turn us on but also communicate essential truths and intimacies about our sexuality, ourselves, and our relationship.

That's not to say that it's easy to get into the habit of using sensual language with our loves. For many women I've worked with, it's even harder to hear such erotic compliments and feedback than to say it.

"I mean, it's like admitting to the animal side of our bodies. It's so personal!" Kalli noted during a private coaching session. "Think about it. I spent my whole pubescent and adult life trying to hide that stuff. I don't want to know that someone can smell my vagina, and I can't believe they would like it if they could. I mean, I know that lovers are supposed to lust over that stuff about each other, but I can't undo a lifetime of learning how to cover, hide, and change my sexual self. I put the radio on so he can't hear my wetness. I turn the lights off so he can't see my flaws or my arousal. I feel like my body is something that betrays me by being dirty and outside my control, especially down there. How in the world am I supposed to come to peace with having to announce how I stimulate their senses, much less what they do to mine?"

It was so hard for Kalli to share this much with me that she asked to turn off her webcam and complete the session by voice only. Simply talking about that level of intimacy felt too vulnerable for her, and I don't blame her.

As women, when it comes to our bodily processes and changes, we're trained to stuff it up, cover it, reshape it, enhance it, get surgery for it, or ignore it and hope that everyone else does the same. It takes many of us years just to process the cruel lunchroom jokes from grade school about our gender and our bodies. Even if we know deep down that they're wrong, we still internalize many of these messages and come to believe them. After all, if we could feel fine about ourselves just as we are, then the advertising industry would be in trouble.

Challenging Bodily Judgments

I have nothing against pampering, caring for, and decorating ourselves, as long as it's inspired by the joy of treating ourselves well instead of the fear that our bodies aren't perfect just as they are. As I discussed with Kalli, it requires a dedicated, ongoing effort for any woman to resist these deeply felt, wildly popular, negative messages propagated by our pasts and our society. I often suggest a four-part exercise when we find ourselves face-to-face with a possible sexist or antisexual block. It's composed of four simple yet deeply probing questions:

Is this a fact or an assumption?

From whom (or where) did I learn this?

Is this information truly in my best interest?

If it's not in my best interest, what new information will I use to replace the faulty assumption?

The first question tackles the negative belief head-on. An assumption doesn't have a clear origin and isn't supported by anything other than your opinion or the opinions of others. It's often based in myth, urban legend, magical thinking, stereotypes, or social control efforts (like those marketing messages that want you to believe you're not good enough as you are). These are the sorts of things about which we might say, "Well, everybody knows that" or "I guess it's something I've always known."

Some assumptions are useful and valuable, but others are damaging and should be replaced with new, better information. Stop to think about any piece of information that's negatively affecting your personal, relational, or sexual goals and well-being. If its status as a supported and research-based fact is shaky, then proceed to the next question.

Where did you learn this damaging assumption? You may not be able to identify precisely when or how you first learned the assumption, but you probably have a vague idea about it or you can recognize where it's been repeated to you. Oftentimes it will quickly become clear that you shouldn't be letting this assumption guide or affect you once you realize where it came from. For example, did you come to feel this way because of something an ex-partner said about you, because your sister or mother was insecure about the same thing, or because you were raised to believe that good women/mothers/wives/daughters/girlfriends had to act in a certain way? If the source of the information seems shoddy or suspicious, then the assumption is probably no better.

Proceed to the next question: Is this information truly in your best interest? Was this information designed to make others more comfortable, wealthier, more powerful, or give them a better quality of life at your expense? When you believe this information, do you take on extra guilt, responsibility, expense, or hassle on yourself that others (especially guys) don't have to worry about?

If this assumption seems to have a negative one-sided effect, then it's certainly not in your best interest. Maybe it doesn't just hurt you; perhaps it also hurts those around you at the same time or affects them because it hurts you. That's another clue that this assumption is not in your best interests.

Finally, now that you've isolated your assumption and decided that you don't want it anymore, it's time to replace it with a new belief or fact that does make your life, sexuality, and relationships better. In the easiest situations, you'll have a strongly ingrained thought habit to break. In more challenging circumstances, this will also mean making changes in your interpersonal relationships to support your new information, like informing your friends or partner that you'll no longer be controlled by the old, negative assumption. The results are always worth it, though. Now you can rejoice in being free of a damaging piece of emotional baggage that you've been carrying for far too long!

Let's consider Kalli's example about the natural scent of her vagina and vulva, especially when she became aroused. A healthy woman's sex organs have a natural scent that ranges from slightly acidic to slightly sweet, depending on where she is in her cycle or if she's already entered menopause. The intensity of her natural scent also varies based on the same factors as well as whether or not she's aroused.

I asked Kalli to consider the first question: Is her belief about her vaginal odor a fact or assumption? Kalli knows that her own scent is natural and normal; she knows how to wash herself appropriately and doesn't have any infections that would contribute to an unpleasant, unhealthy odor. Still, she believes that a woman's natural odor is inherently shameful. Kalli tells me that she doesn't know how she knows—a strong indicator that it's a myth instead of a fact.

She agrees to consider the second question: Where did she learn that vaginas (and especially her vagina) have a gross and embarrassing smell? She can remember the mortifying jokes from as far back as middle school, and her sisters' and stepmother's intimate deodorizing products in the linen closet while she was growing up. She also recalls her own embarrassment when she entered puberty before her peers and had to learn to bathe more often and wear deodorant while still in elementary school; she was terribly ashamed of these changes and felt ostracized by her peers.

After a great deal of thought, she isn't sure exactly where she learned this, and none of the possible sources seem reliable. Although she remains close with her stepmother and sisters, she isn't convinced that they learned this myth from sources that were any better than hers. Her one abusive ex-boyfriend made fun of her for every little mistake or insecurity, yet not even he mentioned this topic! If he had, it wouldn't make it true, of course, but the fact that he didn't made Kalli wonder why she was doing it for him. She isn't ready to let go of her damaging belief yet, but she's become suspicious about it now that she's faced it head-on and begun to think critically about it.

I ask Kalli if this information is in her best interest; does it do more harm than good for her to base relevant decisions around this myth? At first she's adamant that it's useful, because it saves her from embarrassing herself in public and with people in whom she's interested by influencing her to use perfumed products and vaginal cleansers frequently.

Her belief is on shaky ground, though, and she's beginning to wonder if her vagina really deserves to be treated like an unwelcome guest. Has it actually done anything offensive? Aside from being along for the ride when puberty hit, has it actually caused her any embarrassment with others? It turns out that it's her embarrassment that's been hurting her, not her vagina or its imaginary bad odors, as she recounts story after story of lovers who wished she could just relax and enjoy their time together.

Her worries about smell are a perfect match for her concerns that her vulva is also visually unattractive, possibly even misshapen, and an all-around disgraceful part of her body. Many of her partners have asked what they could do to help her relax. Some even commented that they loved it when they could tell she was turned on, a comment that always had the opposite effect for her.

I asked Kalli if every woman she knew put the same amount of time and energy into saving the world from the smell of their lady parts. She laughed and said that some did, but most didn't. She knows this because they don't pack an arsenal of products when they travel with her, and they sometimes share stories of welcoming lovers to explore their taste and smell.

Was Kalli offended by their odor? No, she had never noticed it. Eventually Kalli concluded that there was nothing helpful about her negative beliefs about her vagina and its natural scent and that it was actually creating a lot of stress and hassle for her, and costing money. It was time to let it go.

Kalli decided to take a couple of weeks to consider what she would choose to believe that would actually be useful and helpful to her. She knew she wouldn't automatically switch to her new belief; old habits are hard to break and she'd been in the habit of feeling ashamed of her vulva since childhood. But making the conscious decision to be mindful about catching herself when she had a shaming thought and replacing it with her new one turned out to be worth the effort. A couple of years later she dropped me a note with a photo of her onstage, performing in *The Vagina Monologues*. Appropriately enough, she played the part of a woman who learned to love her vagina with the help of an adoring one-night stand.

Immersing Yourself in Sensual Language

I find that my four myth-busting questions and an increase in sensual language make a powerful combination for women! Each activity seems to help the other, creating a dynamic improvement in both erotic self-esteem and hot talk in the bedroom. Sensual language is a key element to slowing down and getting unstuck in a sexually stale relationship, as well as taking a stalled relationship to a more intimate and erotic level. Simple changes in language are all it takes; the inclusion of sensual talk quickly transforms dirty talk from awkward or generic to intimately intense.

Consider the difference between the following pairs of phrases. In each pair, the first contains no sensual language, while the second includes descriptions based on the senses. Which would make you feel more special (and aroused), or make your partners realize how much you desire them?

1: *Baby, you're so hot. Are you turned on? I'm turned on.*

2: *[Taking a deep breath.] Your scent is intoxicatingly musky; I can smell how turned on you are. Can you feel how wet/hard I am for you, for your scent?*

1: *Oh, I love to touch you so much. I mean, your skin is just so hot and sexy!*

2: *Your skin is smooth, like rich gourmet chocolate melting on my fingers. I love the way your skin becomes softer at your inner thighs. When I starting running my fingers over you right here I can feel you melt for me.*

1: *That's it, moan for me. I love the way you sound when you're turned on!*

2: *When I touch you here, your breath is deep and full. But when I touch you like this, your voice is hot and needy for me. I wonder what you would sound like if I did both at once, like this . . .*

The second phrases are far more personal, with room to make them even more so. They're also longer, because it's easier to say more when we explore sensual details. Generic "that's so hot, you're so sexy" statements ring hollow when compared with personalized, intimate, and sensual language.

Where did these descriptive words come from, and how can you get them to spill from your own lips? For another one of my clients, the key was a bowl of fruit, plus a little mindful concentration on her senses. Jenny called me for the sole purpose of learning to talk dirty. Her relationship was great, she felt good about herself in bed, but one lover after another had asked her to be more verbal, to no avail. After discussing the importance of honest, authentic dirty talk, we launched straight into one of my favorite sensual talk activities: exploring the five senses with fruit.

I asked her to pick out some of her favorite fruit between this session and the next, and to eat it slowly and mindfully. While she enjoyed it, I wanted her to jot down descriptions for each bite under all five senses: taste, touch, sight, smell, and sound. (You'll find my "Sensual Language Guide" for this activity in Chapter 12, so you can follow along for yourself!) A few days later, Jenny sent the following list:

Strawberries: rough to touch, sweet and tart, juicy, crunchy noise, tiny hard seeds, deep red, dense, refreshing

Blueberries: smooth to touch, sweet and tart, juicy, round, tiny, deep blue

Blackberries: soft to touch, bursting, mild flavor, sweet, soft texture, velvety, dark, bumpy, fluffy

At our next scheduled call I asked Jenny how it was different eating the fruit for homework, compared with her usual fruit salad with lunch. She responded that it made her focus on an activity that she usually does mechanically and without thinking, giving her more appreciation for something that she's been doing for years. Jenny hadn't really noticed all of the textures of berries before and was now more aware of their shapes, color variations, and feel in her mouth.

Eating the fruit was more enjoyable, and she now thinks of the berries differently when she eats them, because she's more aware of them. They even look different, as she pays more attention to their color, ripeness, and the promise of a juicy treat to be savored slowly. It's as though the berries want her attention, and not just to be eaten as a matter of habit. By the end of her description we were both chuckling to ourselves. These are the exact same things we all want for our sex lives, too!

I asked her to picture the fruit in her mind and consider it with me again, so that we could expand her excellent list a bit further. Starting with sight, I suggested that she tell me about the first moment that she laid eyes on the fruit, knowing that she'd pay more attention to it this time. I took notes as she spoke to me about how the berries stimulated her sense of sight, encouraging her to flesh out her words into phrases and sentences. This is what she said:

> *I opened the refrigerator door and thought, "Oh, I'd like to have that." As I rinsed the berries, the water washed over the fruit, making the skin shiny and wet. I realized that it was as though I was giving the fruit a shower. One of the berries was calling to me, so I picked it up. It was plump, firm, and I was filled with anticipation because it was going to taste delicious. The color was bright and deep, calling me to eat it first. The texture of the fruit's skin looked smooth and I wanted to feel it in my mouth. It was the exact right ripeness, letting me know that it was ready for me. I knew there would be a ripe, burst of flavor that would come from biting into it and I thought, "This is going to be juicy!"*

If that isn't dirty talk, I don't know what is! In fact, our conversation was so steamy that I've compiled her thoughts on every taste and included them with other real-life dirty talk examples in Chapter 13. Flip to that chapter any time you need a little inspiration of your own!

The more Jenny shared, the more apparent it was that this sensual talk could easily cross over into direct, sexually charged dirty talk with her lover. But, before racing to that level, she needed to practice so that her vocal intonations were suggestive, the words flowed freely, and she felt more confident. She decided to begin by sharing her thoughts about the fruit with her lover, exactly as we wrote them. At the end, she would simply add "and I was thinking of you." This tiny addition let her partner know that Jenny was thinking about him in sensual ways, without pushing her to do anything more than describe her experiences with the fruit.

Key Points

- Sensual language is the key to hot, personalized talk, as well as an expansive and evolving dirty talk vocabulary.
- To appreciate all of the senses, you must also appreciate your own body and your sexual responses. Take the time to explore and process any negative messages you have about your body, especially your most intimate areas, so that you can give and receive sensual language freely.
- Beginning with enjoying sensual items, such as fruit, is an excellent way to build your sensual language skills.

EXERCISE

Turn to the "Sensual Language Guide" in Chapter 12 and grab a piece of fruit! Soon you'll be crafting naughty whispers over each bite that can turn into seductive messages for your lover.

NINE

Three Levels of Dirty Talk

Cameryn: You want me to squirt? Then you better get two
fingers up in my cunt and find that spot on the
roof of my pussy, you know where it is. Work
it, baby, work it good. That's right, THAT'S
RIGHT, OH MY GOD, YES YES YES YES, OH MY
GOD, OH MY GOD, OH GOD OH GOD OH GOD
OH GOD DON'T YOU STOP . . . and the wetness
spurts out in two or three splashes across your
mouth and chin. Don't stop. Don't you dare stop.
Drink it up. Drink it all up.

(Eric comes.)

Cameryn: Mmmmm . . . So. You still only good, or did we
get you up to awesome?

Jenny, from the previous chapter, might have been thinking of
her boyfriend, but she was still working her magic by talking
about innocent pieces of fruit. Innocent as the berries may be,
calling to her from their bowl after their bath, her words were
anything but. She'd discovered the first of my three levels of
dirty talk, and it only gets naughtier from there! By dividing
dirty talk into a progression of three categories, you'll find that
you're more able to ease into talking dirty to your partners
with hot confidence and plenty of inspiration.

Some nice girls decide to go all the way and learn to comfortably move between all three levels. Others of us will find
our favorite level and stay there, because that's what works

for us. This is not a race to the nastiest finish! Find the level or levels that turn you on and enjoy exploring them with your partners for as long as you like. Those who enjoy all three levels should also remember that sometimes the first and second steps are the most appropriate and seductive, even if the third is the naughtiest.

When it comes to talking dirty, by exploring and having fun with it you'll discover that there's a natural progression of naughtiness. The most basic, sensual, and intimate level is the least explicit, not because the words are any less sexual but because it's based on describing inanimate objects, like fruit. In the previous chapter, you learned how Jenny's experience of eating fruit became more enjoyable when she made a point of being aware of her senses throughout the experience. It also yielded a hot list of descriptors that turned into a smoldering script for talking dirty to her sweetheart.

This is a beautiful way to build comfort and communication skills while stoking the flames of lust, whether you're shy or bold. Even my most nervous clients can bite into an apple and describe the act to me as they're chewing on the crisp flesh. After we've developed a rich narrative of their experience with the apple, their faces light up as they realize that they've just crafted a delightful dirty talk script without much, if any, discomfort!

Beginning dirty talkers often voice the concern that they're being too cognitive and aren't thinking sexy thoughts at all during the exercise. Even Jenny, who ended with quite a naughty result on her first try, didn't realize the sexually charged nature of her words until partway into the activity. That's the wonderful thing about beginning at the beginning: It's nearly foolproof. The joy of a successful experience, and the recognition (even after the fact) that you crafted a delicious piece of oral seduction, will help you be more mindful of the activity's erotic side next time.

During this level of dirty talk you have the opportunity to create a new story for yourself as an erotic woman: You're a deeply sexual being with the ability to communicate erotically, whether or not you know it. With a little more practice, you'll be able to amend that story into that of a woman who can easily express her sexual side anytime she likes. Take a few moments to breathe in that image of yourself, picturing and feeling yourself as a woman well on her way to being the kind of person who emanates sexual energy with confidence, grace, and skill.

For women who fancy themselves cognitive thinkers, with an emphasis on thoughts and facts over feelings, this is your time to shine. Your ability to break a situation down into its various components is a strong asset for this level of dirty talk. Some time ago, a very cognitive gentleman still dressed in a bland business suit surprised our entire workshop by blundering into an amazingly seductive statement. Kristian stared thoughtfully at his berry, never breaking eye contact with it, while he calmly and clearly stated,

> *I'm most aware of the way my strawberry gives itself to the pressure of my lips and teeth. The skin of the fruit resists me at first, then gives in to my teeth as it yields softly to my pressure. It isn't objecting, though, because it rewards me with its sweetly scented juice as though it is inviting me, teasing me, into doing it again.*

The room stared at him in awed silence. I believe I can speak for everyone there when I say that he was transforming before our very eyes. His gray suit and loosened tie shifted from signals of a rushed office worker to an intriguing image of tousled professionalism. His factual, quiet manner had taken on a certain aura of sensuality, as though he could see things about us that we hadn't known before meeting him.

"Yes, I suppose that was a bit dirty sounding, wasn't it? I guess I did it right, after all," he added with a laugh, in response to our wide-eyed awe. He was one of the last participants to leave at the end of the night, accompanied by a lovely woman he had met at the event. Cognitive thinkers, proud nerds if you will, often know that they could be fantastic lovers if they could only turn their whirring brains into engines of sexiness. My dear, cognitive lovers, let loose your carefully nurtured brains and entice us with your disarmingly honest attention to detail. We want to imagine what it would be like if you paid the same attention to our words and maybe even our bodies!

Level One: Describing Objects

This first level of dirty talk, describing objects, is the perfect time to use a simple yet powerful phrase that I mentioned already: "and I was thinking of you." It's essential that you tie your sensation-based language back to the object of your affection through words, intonation, body language, or all three. A phrase like this builds a bridge between the cognitive nature of your description and your erotic goals. Kristian did it unintentionally when he gazed up at the circle of women around him with a self-conscious blush that confirmed that he was coming to the same realization as we were about what he just said out loud. If your style of seduction is sweet, innocent, shy, corruptible, or playful, then Kristian's body language might be the perfect way for you to convey your seductive intent.

For those with a more direct dirty talking style, a similarly direct bridge may be necessary to ensure that we get our point across. Jenny got so absorbed in describing her fruit salad that she wasn't even aware of her flirtatious potential. For Jenny, knowing that she'd end her dirty talk script with the "and I was thinking of you" bridge also helped make her more aware of her own erotic energy.

Another helpful thing about a bridge like that is that it doesn't demand a response from your partner or a follow-up comment from you. Simply wink, smile, blush, or gently change the topic when you're done. If your partner is too surprised or shy to respond, it doesn't ruin the moment. Good introductory dirty talk is able to stand on its own, giving everyone involved the chance to appreciate it, ponder it, and decide how to respond. Whether you use this as a light form of drive-by dirty talk or an advanced, interactive style of seduction, level one is able to meet your goals.

Begin by yourself with fruit, chocolate, creamy coffee, wine, or whatever you enjoy imbibing slowly. Write down your words and phrases with a pen and paper (typing and screens can kill sensuality in this kind of activity) organized by sense. Make time to return to them the next day and flesh out your words as you remember your sensual experience.

Practice saying them aloud before slipping snippets into text messages, voice mails, e-mails, or a naughty whisper over drinks. When you feel ready, invite your sweetheart to join you for a picnic in the park or the middle of your bed. Be sure to pack a range of light morsels, a washable blanket, and a little pack of baby wipes because you won't be including utensils. Enjoy the fun and sexiness of feeding each other by hand as you take turns describing each bite to each other, one sense at a time. If you're feeling particularly bold, you can use this as a transition point to the second level by occasionally comparing your delicacies to attributes about each other.

Level Two: Describing Your Attributes

The first level is the best introduction to dirty talk exercises, because even the shyest nice girls can muster the courage to describe a fruit and follow it up with an adorable blush or wink. Level two makes the jump to direct, personalized dirty talk by focusing on attributes of yourself and your partner. This level can include descriptive talk about physical characteristics, areas of the body, personality facets, and other aspects of yourself or your partner. That's right, now we're talking about everything from their sexy laugh to the perfect curves of your derriere.

Although it's easier to use tame language at this level, the intimate nature of the conversation makes it much more personal and intimate. This level is the place to offer heartfelt, naughty (or feigned-innocent) compliments, build emotional and physical intimacy through your shared sexual energy, and learn a great deal more about what you both enjoy about each other. For those who are shy, stick with the first level until you're comfortable, and you'll eventually find yourself effortlessly wandering into level two without realizing it.

Level two capitalizes on the sensual skills you learned with fruit in level one, but applies it to your lover and yourself. Now you're describing attributes of yourself and your lover through sight, touch, smell, sound, and taste. This can be a lusciously vulnerable experience for everyone involved. The act of bluntly expressing our lust for our partners can also be incredibly erotic by stripping away our pretenses and social graces, leaving us both physically and emotionally naked. What a wonderful time to cover each other in seductive, erotic, and uplifting language!

If you find yourself intimidated by this prospect, return to Chapter 8 and consider Kalli's concerns with sensual language about her body. This may ring true for you, or at least help you understand where your own block is coming from at this level. It may also not be time yet, or ever, and that's fine, too. Remember, each level is perfect on its own, and there's no need to push yourself to the next level to be a better lover, more sexual, or any of the other comparisons we make about ourselves.

Most of the women I work with report that this level feels natural after plenty of practice, and perhaps some processing of emotional blocks that reared their inconvenient heads. What makes this level so attractive and honest is rooted in our desire to convey our attraction to our partners. We all learn cultural scripts and rules for how to do this in socially appropriate ways. It's appropriate to hold each other's hands to demonstrate our affection and enjoyment of the feeling of each other's skin, and young lovers may even walk with their hands in each other's rear pockets. But someone would probably call the police if you communicated that joy by walking around with your hands in each others' flies!

We frown on people who say "I love you" or "I want to have sex with you" too soon, even if it would be an honest statement. But being too verbally withdrawn is just as likely to send your dating partners running the other way. Countless books have been written for women on how to successfully navigate the convoluted rules of communication during dating. What a relief to strip all of that away by immersing yourself in this level! Throw away all the crazy complexity and simply describe directly what attracts you to your lover and what you'd like them to be attracted to in you.

After her experience with the berries, I asked Jenny to think of one of her favorite parts of her boyfriend's body. She immediately picked his chest, and so I asked her to use the same process to explore how his chest stimulates her senses. She described everything from the sensation of running her fingertips through the silvery hair on his chest and tummy to the smell of his cologne and its impact on her.

She felt that he probably knew that she liked his chest because she'd mentioned it, and she also liked to spend a lot of time snuggling against his torso. But she'd never taken the time to directly tell him. It wasn't for lack of trying! She admitted to being on the verge of telling him several times, only to lose her words and end up feeling silly as he hugged her.

As I reminded Jenny, this level can be very complimentary, but it isn't about making compliments. This is a selfish level that's all about showing off your descriptive skills. But instead of starting with a clumsy "I really like your . . . ," pick a sense and describe it: "The curve at the side of your hip catches the light from outside just so, drawing my eye over your skin to the pool of light at your inner thigh."

Your lovers will recognize that your thoughts are complimentary, but, even better, they'll understand that you're personalizing your lust and attraction. Pointing out how your eyes move over your lovers' body is charged with erotic symbolism and the promise of a similarly lingering touch. Whether they blush or puff with pride, deep down they want to hear more. So don't stop there.

Continue with the same sense and a different attribute, or the same attribute but a different sense. Changing both the attribute and the sense right away can result in a disconnected muddle of comments that lacks flow. Let's stick with the sense of sight and the light from the window, but change the attribute. The next comment may be something like, "And yet your breast is in the shadow; I can barely see it except where your nipple catches the light again, right here. It's as though it wants my attention, too."

For a male partner who entices your sense of smell, you might begin by nuzzling his hair, saying, "Your hair smells gritty, yet clean. I can smell a hint of your shampoo and it makes me think of you in the shower. I like that thought as much as I like burying my face in your hair." After pausing to appreciate the scent of his hair, you might move down his body and continue with the same sense: "But at the back of your neck there is just a hint of fresh sweat left over from the gym. It's musky and deep, with a touch of bitterness that makes me want to taste you." And now you're ready to switch to the sense of taste, if you want to.

Speak slowly and mindfully, matching the tone of your voice to your dirty talk style and character. Your vocal inflection says as much about your partner and yourself as your words do. Technically, you're making a descriptive list of your thoughts, based on your senses. But what you're communicating is much richer and more meaningful.

Remember how your dirty talk character talks and moves when she's flirting instead of concentrating on her descriptive vocabulary during a steamy moment. Bring the essences of that character to your dirty talk to help you feel more natural and authentic to yourself and your desires. If you find yourself feeling shy or lost, back up to flirting in-character and playfully tease your way forward again once you're comfortable. Or it may all come so naturally that you haven't thought about channeling your character, since you invited your lover to help you with your zipper.

Level Three: Desires, Actions, and Corresponding Sensations

If level two became personal and intimate by making a giant leap to describing each other's attributes, brace yourself! Level three focuses on your lustiest desires, your bodies in motion, and the sensations elicited by those motions. You're still practicing the same trusty descriptive skills, often focusing on the senses, but this level transitions to more tangible focal points. Like the move from the first to the second level, most of the women I work with report that moving to level three feels surprisingly natural after they've explored and built confidence with the second level.

This is your opportunity to get graphically explicit, by using adverbs as much as adjectives. I've often heard that this level taps into the animalistic, unguarded element of sexual energy. It's a side that many lovers simultaneously pursue and back away from, recognizing its desirability while fearing the feeling of losing their self-control to lust. Women who experience this deeper, more fulfilling sexual energy sometimes report that their moans have changed from gasps to snarls, screams, and growls! If this is what you're hoping for, then allowing yourself to tap into the potential of level three may be just the thing.

We've broken social rules by openly sharing our sensual experience of each other's bodies. We've thought of how to say where your eyes lingered on her body and to describe that musky smell at the base of his neck. But what does it make you want to do? If you're already doing it, what is it that you're doing? And how does it feel to be doing it? At level three we stop hiding behind the word *it* to say exactly what you're talking about and how it feels to all of your senses.

Fantasies, needs, and intense body language are all a part of this level. But it remains grounded in sensual talk as the basis for intimate, honest, and creative dirty talk. Illustrative comparisons can be tempting as you gain practice at level three, but don't succumb to them any more than absolutely necessary. They offer a convenient place to hide from the pull of that deeper sexual energy by creating a shortcut around descriptive language.

If your lover were to look up during oral sex and say, "Sinking my tongue into your vulva is like biting into a ripe slice of orange," it may create an image in your mind, but what does your lover mean? What are they trying to say about the experience, exactly? Instead, your lover should consider what the experience has in common with biting into a ripe orange, and then describe it:

When my tongue sinks into your vulva I can feel your wetness flowing into my mouth and covering my lips as your layers part for me. Your taste is intoxicating, filling, and I can't get enough. I want to bury myself in you, feel you all over me, until there is nothing left but your scent, your taste, your slick wetness.

Now you know exactly what your lover is experiencing, feeling, and thinking. We're not interested in letting our partners fill in the gaps with their imagination when we talk dirty: We want them to know exactly what we're sensing, wanting, and doing.

Take the opportunity to flex your dirty talk skills by describing what you want to do:

I'm looking at your body in the glow from the street light outside your window, and I want to trace my finger over each smooth, glowing curve at your inner thigh. I want to find out if your skin gets softer where the light fades away.

The way your neck smells, musky and salty, makes me wonder what you'd taste like if I opened my lips on your skin and pressed my tongue against the back of your neck.

If the reaction is positive, follow through by doing exactly what you just described. Be sure to describe your movements and their response. You can also describe what you'd like to do next, paving the way for your next bit of dirty talk:

I can feel you throbbing as I wrap my hand around you. Oh, when I squeeze a little you throb for me even more! You're so hot to the touch right now, maybe I should find something slick and wet to cover you.

I can't believe how deep and strong your body is around my hand. It's as though I can feel all of you right here. I can feel every move, every moan right here around my hand. I want to know what happens when I turn my fingers like this.

Don't forget to use this level of dirty talk to describe what it's like to be pleasured by your partner, too! You may have trouble finding your words if they're doing a good job, but it's worth the effort, and the breaks in your voice will make it even sexier.

As you can see, the third level has incredible potential for becoming as dirty and direct as you dare. In addition to the use of sense-based language, it still shares an important aspect with the first level. When we stop to appreciate and express our sexuality, and that of our partners, we enjoy it more. Jenny doesn't look at her fruit salad the same anymore, and even when she's in a rush it still tastes better than it used to. When she's getting hungry in the late morning, she thinks about those berries and anticipates eating them first. It's the same with intensely intimate dirty talk; we find ourselves more aware of our shared sexual energy, we daydream about it in new ways, and we encourage each other to explore in new ways. Sex need never become stale or routine with sensuality and communication skills like these!

Key Points

- Describing inanimate objects is the first level of dirty talk. It's incredibly sensual and can be quite seductive once you build a bridge between the object and your sweetie. Try finishing your description with "and I was thinking of you."
- Describing attributes is the next level. It's more personal, but still based in sensual language. It also allows you to

build sensual intimacy by sharing what you love about yourself and your partner.

- Describing desires, actions, and sensations is the third and most intense level. Sensual language remains key at this level, but it's dirtier than the other two because it has the potential to be the most explicit. Remember, the more explicit it is, the greater the opportunity to build intensely sexual emotional intimacy, as well as aural pleasure!
- Don't push yourself beyond your comfort level. Each step can be a great complement to your love life, but pressuring yourself will likely lead to an unpleasant experience.

EXERCISE

Choose an indirect form of communication, such as e-mail, text messages, or even a phone conversation, and begin to explore one step at a time. Stop when you feel that the intensity stretches your boundaries just a bit, without making you unpleasantly uncomfortable. Be sure to invite your partner to respond in kind, but don't feel pressured to match each other's levels, if they differ.

TEN

Discover Fantasies

Cameryn: Let me get down there and get that all slicked up. First I'm going to gently brush your ball sac with my fingertips, so smooth and light. Does that feel good?

Jason: Ohhh… you makin' me shiver, baby.

Cameryn: Mmmm. Maybe get my lips under there and just lick and kiss you all around on your balls. (slurping noises) Mmmm, god. I can feel your cock getting all heavy and hard against my cheek.

Jason: Oh, yeah.

Sensual descriptions of objects, attributes, desires, actions, and sensations are an exciting way to explore dirty talk. By gaining experience and confidence, you can choose to move through the various levels, or stop where you're comfortable and enjoy your favorite level of dirty talk as much as you like. So far we've explored nonfiction dirty talk, focusing on our sensations and venturing forth from there while staying grounded in the present (or at least the realistic). Dirty talk doesn't need to end there; the possibilities are as wide as your imagination, as long as you're enjoying yourself! Whether they're softly seductive or rough and wild, fantasies and dirty talk are perfect together.

While fantasy building deserves its own book, I would be remiss if I didn't include a basic foundation for how to enhance dirty talk with a twist of fantasies. By learning about the three basic levels of verbal fantasy—building on the past, forecasting the future, and inviting original fantasies—you'll be on your way to blending fact and fantasy into delightful verbal scenarios. Unlike the three levels of dirty talk, these do not get progressively more intense. Instead, they get more creative as you move through each level.

Building on the Past

The place to begin, they say, is at the beginning. Perhaps you were a nice girl with a naughty side when you were younger, chasing the boys or inviting them to chase you. Maybe you kept yourself busy with other things, but watched with envy, whether or not you admitted it. Or you may have been more like me, blissfully naive about all the fuss until years after my friends had launched excitedly into the sexual unknown. Oh well, we're catching up now, aren't we?

The first level of fantasy creation involves re-creating the past to give yourself the chance to relive it with a bit more abandon. This is still based somewhat in reality, in that you're taking inspiration from earlier years (yours or someone else's) and then bringing those memories to the present. Most of us have heard talk show hosts recommend that established couples pretend to meet each other at the bar for the first time, picking each other up as though they were a fresh fling instead of steady lovers. This is the perfect example of the first level.

We're never too old, or too long in our relationships, to try a bit of kissing and petting in the back of the movie theater! This type of fantasy play harkens back to the wanton exploration often found at the beginning of relationships, or the beginning of our sexual development, depending on how far back you take your fantasy play. The act of flirting, the zest of uncertainty and anticipation, and the joy of exploring each other as though for the first time is a potent mix.

For those who dare, this type of dirty talk can accompany a bit of role-play by creating and acting out your own sexy piece of theater. Or you may simply imagine along with each other as your dialogue creates a delightful story that might even inspire you to play along as you get the good parts. For those of you who tell a good story, put your narrative skills to work and share a favorite sexy memory from earlier in your relationship or from before you met your sweetie, and embellish along the way.

Take some time to yourself, or with your sweetie if it won't make you too shy, and reminisce about your saucy past adventures. This is not the time for jealousy over past relationships, if you're sharing together. All of us have different sexual paths during our lifetimes, and there's absolutely nothing wrong with remembering past crushes, romances, and lovers fondly. Remember that each of you has now chosen each other because that's whom you want to be with.

As with all dirty talk, the richest, most intimate descriptions are based in the senses. Although you may be describing a date that never actually happened (or a better version of the real thing), you should still use sensual language as the basis of your dirty talk. Take a look at these two examples; the first uses level one fantasy language, but no sensual language. I think you'll agree that the second one is more like what you'd want to hear or say.

Remember the way we use to explore each other for hours? I couldn't get enough of touching you, and you never wanted me to stop.

Remember the way I used to run my fingers over your skin, slowly circling in on your favorite places? I would draw my fingers along the edge of your panties, just like this, and you knew that I was pushing the edge back just a bit, like this, but you'd pretend not to notice. I loved the way your skin becomes so soft, smooth, and sensitive right here where your inner thigh meets your body. As much as I wanted to look at your body, I couldn't help but look up at your eyes instead, like I am now. The way your lashes fluttered and you caught your breath like so. I had to watch your face and wait for you to open your eyes and meet mine.

The first example is over too quickly, and it doesn't give enough detail to make it hot. It's more of a fond memory than a piece of dirty talk. In the second example, the speaker is using sensual language to describe the past while enacting the memory at the same time. They're simply describing what they did, using sensual details, and doing it at the same time. This kind of dirty talk could easily last throughout your time together without being boring or causing a loss for words. You can also adjust it to fit your personal style and character by adjusting the tone (of both your words and your voice) and the explicitness of your language.

Remember that building on the past is an opportunity to embellish, re-create, and even come up with original fantasies. The commonality is that we take inspiration from our real or imagined pasts, and the rush of intense passion that comes with an early time in our relationships or our lives. This is just the inspiration, though, not the boundaries! Build forward from there in any and every way that pleases you.

Forecasting the Future

The easiest way to start a fantasy is to begin with what you know or what you wish you knew. The former works because it has a familiar basis, the latter works because you've already spent quite a bit of time thinking about it. And if you can reimagine and create new stories for your past, then it's only a small step toward creating fantasies of what you might do in the future. In fact, the vast majority of women have already been raised to be skilled at this! Whether we imagined our own weddings or just listened to our friends as they shared their romantic fantasies of wedded bliss, eventually someone in our group of young female friends probably started sharing her thoughts on the wedding night.

In these fantasies, bachelorette parties full of tawdry gifts meet special white lingerie, and a romance novel begins building in many women's imaginations. Even if you didn't participate in those daydreams, you probably were socialized to be good at this just in case you wanted to. This is just one of many examples of forecasting the future as a type of fantasy, with ripe potential for dirty talk.

This form of dirty talk can also refer to a few hours or minutes from now, instead of years. Lydia shared one of her tips after a recent workshop.

When Jacob comes home from work, sex is usually the last thing on his mind even if it's the first thing on mine. He works very hard and his commute is pretty wicked, whereas I work from home as often as not. I'm ready to celebrate the end of the workday, especially on Friday, but sometimes his mind is still churning with work stuff. This used to bother me a lot and led to some frustrated spats. One day on his way home from work I gave him a call to check on when he might get in. I happened to be folding laundry, so when he asked what I was doing I mentioned that I was hanging up a piece of lingerie. He misunderstood me and thought I was selecting it to wear, not putting it away. So I ran with it and began to tell him how naughty we could be together if he hurried home to find me in it. Our minds were definitely in the same place when he walked in the door! Now I sometimes give him a call as he gets out of work and try a little flirting. If he isn't in the mood, I change the subject. If he seems interested, then I'll start talking dirty with him, to help him get in the mood along with me.

As Lydia discovered, using dirty talk to predict exciting future sex can be a great way to make it happen. This is especially useful with partners who seem to have trouble finding times when they're both interested; someone always seems to feel playful when the other isn't. There are various reasons why some couples can't seem to get their schedules to match when it comes to sex, but no matter what the cause, it can be useful to slow down and help your lovers catch up to your arousal level if they want to. I've met many, many clients who have told me that they may not be in the mood when their lover approaches them for sex, but they'd be willing to be seduced if their partner would just slow down and help them get there.

Forecasting future sexual activity is also a fantastic way to gauge interest and consent erotically. Long-distance lovers know this trick well. Those who live across the country, or across oceans, often discover the importance of maintaining a sexy relationship over the phone. If you could see your sweetie only a few times every year, I'm sure you'd get creative, too!

As visits get closer, these couples will often enjoy imagining how they'll pleasure each other when they're together again. They may suggest new activities and explore them over the phone many times first, helping make it less of a jolt when they move to that level in person. Even those who don't live across distances can benefit from this: Many people find it easier to spring kinky new ideas by text message or phone than in person. It just doesn't feel as risky, and you can plan your request in advance.

A word of caution with this approach to fantasies, though: Not everyone will want to make these fantasies real, and not every fantasy is as good in real life as it was in your imagination. Although this can also happen with the first level of fantasies, levels two and three are particularly prone to messy miscommunication when it comes to living them out.

After you have fun talking about it, wait a day or two. During a calm time when neither of you is talking dirty nor is upset about anything, directly ask your sweetie if they'd like to try something like what you talked about. Then discuss how you might realistically attempt part or all of it.

Remember, sharing a fantasy and even sharing pleasure in it is never an obligation to try to make it real. You may also want to simply keep your fantasy in your imaginations. Many fantasies are hottest this way, and there's nothing wrong with that!

Inviting Original Fantasies

The wildest possibilities exist when we let our imaginations roam. Sometimes they lead us to sexual frontiers ripe for exploration, other times they teach us about our turn-ons in ways that are better left to the imagination. Original fantasies, those not based in the past or likely future events, can take a myriad of forms. They range from sensation-based fantasies to adoration for certain clothing, props, or gear, to fantastical situations involving new or additional partners. These fantasies often involve an element of power play: one partner (or more) having some sort of power or advantage over the other or others, from subtle to extreme.

A very good friend of mine once confided that he and his wife had threesomes almost every night, yet had never had an additional partner in their bed. After a few drinks he had discovered that they both shared the same vivid fantasy: the desire for a sexy, powerful man to sexually pleasure her while my friend either looked on or helped stimulate her. Although she was shy to admit the idea again later, he was dedicated to seeing if they might be able to reinvigorate their sex life with this shared fantasy. During their lovemaking he would spin delicious stories, tell her wanton dirty tales that turned them both on. Sometimes he'd describe how the other man was looking at her with lust while touching her, or how they were both enjoying her.

In reality it was him touching his wife along with the story, as best he could. But his dirty talk and their imaginations made up for the lack of an extra person, and he found that this kind of play awakened a new sexual energy in her. And they never had to worry about the real-life concerns of finding and integrating a third partner. There was no jealousy, no complicated sexual choreography, no scheduling hassles, and no health risks. Instead, they could leap right into lots of hot, sexy lovemaking between two spouses and their talented imaginary friend!

Fantasy talk at this level, just like all hot fantasy talk, remains based in sensual language. For my friend and his wife, his ability to describe their imaginary lover's facial expressions, muscles, and movements was essential to the success of their dirty talk escapades. Explicit, sensual details offer more to talk about and more to imagine, and make it a personalized experience instead of a generic one. It's just as important to keep your dirty talk style and character in mind. This will make it easier to create delightful scripts and directions that feel authentic and honestly turn on both you and your partner.

Bringing Fantasies to Life

If you decide to try to live out all or part of a fantasy, regardless of which of these three levels you want to try, it helps to put some time into planning. Bringing a fantasy to life can be a particularly vulnerable experience, making it ripe for increased intimacy if it goes well and disappointment if it does not. A well-developed vision of what you want and clear communication with your partner will go a long way toward making it a positive experience. That clear communication is at its best when it includes lots of juicy, dirty talk!

As important as planning is, it's equally essential not to overplan your torrid experience together. I've met many a couple (usually women with men who like to tinker, but it could happen to anyone) in which one or both of them has gotten so wrapped up in planning it's become a stressful performance instead of a pleasure. Costumes have been secured, accents practiced, and every prop has been carefully researched and ordered online.

As they describe their preparations to me, I get the distinct feeling that the rendezvous will be completely ruined if someone skips ahead on the script or decides they'd prefer a different sex act. When I bring up this concern, one of the partners is often relieved to admit to having the same worry, but didn't want to throw a wrench in the works by mentioning it to their overzealous lover.

Planning a good fantasy, whether it's purely verbal or a role-play, means bringing in just enough detail to let your imagination take care of the rest. The sexiest fantasy schoolgirl doesn't need an official uniform with Mary Janes, desk, ruler, backpack, note from home, remote-control vibrator, long pigtails with fluffy elastics, and six pencil cases concealing the perfect glittery dildos and lubes. Spend some time exploring this fantasy through dirty talk (I recommend lots of phone sex), and then reflect on the parts of the dialogue that really got you both off.

If you and your partner's fantasies revolve around sliding off your puritanical panties in the principal's office, then there's no need to include extra props and other complexities. A simple plaid skirt and white cotton panties, and perhaps a lunch box full of naughty goodies, will work just as well and be less difficult to coordinate than a full ensemble. You'll have plenty to inspire dirty language, without feeling as though you're trying to follow a movie script that leaves no room for an ad-libbed conversation or sudden, lusty impulses. The most important thing is that you enjoy yourselves and have fun, so balance your planning with that sense of inspired freedom.

I suggest that those interested in fantasy use a worksheet I've developed to help figure out what they like and then communicate it to a potential partner (or two, or eight . . .). I still suggest starting with lots of dirty talk, but this helps span the gap between the limitless nature of explicit conversations and the reality of lived-out dirty talk. You'll find the worksheet, "Fantasies for the Shy," in Chapter 12. The first thing is to determine the plot. This should be one to three sentences that briefly describe the fantasy's main idea. Here are a few examples:

> *I walk into the locker room to discover the women's swim team getting ready for practice. They're using the lockers near mine, and I try to slip in and watch them unnoticed, but they realize I'm sneaking peeks as they change. The head of the team leads the women in insisting that I put my hands where my eyes are, and I'm embarrassed and thrilled at the same time.*

> *My sweetie comes home unexpectedly to surprise me with lunch, only to find me exploring myself with a vibrator I secretly purchased earlier in the week. He pauses and watches me through a crack in the door as I pleasure myself, and then quietly enters and helps me to another orgasm with my new toy.*

> *I find my honey looking at a porn movie when he thinks I'm busy. He's absolutely mortified and tries to hide the video, but I know what I saw him watching. I "punish"*

him by having him do all the things he's just watched with me for our own video camera.

The second part is the mood. If you think carefully about your plot, you'll sense a tone or mood involved. In the first example, it already says that the woman feels both embarrassed and thrilled. In the second example, you may feel wanton, shy, curious, or lusty while your partner feels any of those emotions or more. In the third, the partner who's been caught feels guilty and "mortified" but may also feel aroused at being caught, while the other partner feels powerful, sexually energized, or any of a wide range of other emotions. These are all possible moods for your time together.

How will your mood be expressed? The words and sensations convey your mood to each other. It's not usually necessary to work out a full script, but certain phrases or sensations may give your fantasy extra zest.

Let's say that you really get turned on by hearing your partner tell you that you're "delicious and wet." Be sure to write those exact words here! Maybe you want to feel your lover's chest rub against yours. Write it down and make sure they know. If you aren't doing the fantasy in real life, you'll still enjoy hearing about those special details during your dirty talk!

Finally, your fantasy should have a culmination, some sort of sexual act or other source of pleasure that you've been working up to. The options for this are as wide as your imagination, so have fun! Remember, intercourse and orgasm are only two possible ways to enjoy the fruits of your fantasy. Pick whatever turns you on most to think about or experience at the end of your naughty adventure.

Key Points

- Building on the past is a powerful, yet less intimidating, way to ease into fantasy talk and play.
- Forecasting the future adds an intense element to fantasy talk by adding anticipation.
- Inviting original fantasies is your opportunity to be as creative as you like and experience your wildest dirty talk together as you indulge your erotic imagination.
- Remember that some fantasies are best kept private, others are meant to be shared but not enacted, and some are the perfect opportunity to become a bit wilder by trying out parts of them. Sharing a fantasy is giving a gift of intimacy, whether or not you both decide you want to talk dirty about it or give it a try together.

EXERCISE

Turn to "Fantasies for the Shy," my guide to exploring and communicating fantasies. Each fantasy should have a plot, mood, or sensations, and a culminating act of pleasure. Offer a worksheet to your lover and then see what each of you has written!

ELEVEN

Dirty Talk for Exploration, Play, and Intimacy

Cameryn: Yeah? Mmmm. I love how you smell down there. And when your balls get all tight like that, I know you're going to give me a really big load at the end, aren't you?

Jason: So fucking big.

Cameryn: Mmmm. (more slurping noise) Let me bathe your balls with my tongue, one at a time, so warm and velvety wet. Do you have precum already? Cuz I want to taste it. Oh, yeah. Just stick my tongue out and pick up that clear little drop, mmmm, tastes so good!

Jason: I'm gonna give you a lot more than that in a little bit.

Now that you're an expert at your personal style of dirty talk, with a vast vocabulary, a solid structure, and a mind full of fantasies, it's time to refocus on how to shape your seduction into playful relationship enhancement. A healthy, happy, and creative sex life can remind us of how important it is to continue to play with our sweeties. It's time we encourage ourselves and each other to invite playfulness and fun back into our relationships, starting with a sassy bit of verbal seduction and sparring. Sexuality is the most intimate form of body language we have; make sure you're using it to build your relationship in sexy, healthy ways.

At the heart of dirty talk is a combination of mindful sensuality and intimately authentic communication. These are skills for seduction, lovemaking, fantasy creation, and arousal, as well as the basics of daily life. While it's not as exciting to think of using these techniques for enjoying road trips, Chase, a close friend of mine, made a good point when he told me about one of the things he appreciates most about his spouse, Rosa:

> *I love taking road trips with her, because she always notices beautiful things that others miss. She pauses to point out sunsets, city views at night, ornately flowered weeds, and even fancy shoes on other women. If I don't understand what makes those things special at first, she draws my attention to their uniqueness until I get it. She's a good communicator like that. I remember one of our first times together, when she stopped to compliment my body and make me feel good about it. She meant it, too. I've never forgotten. Her words still make me feel sexy and confident, years later.*

Two things stood out to me when Chase shared this story. The first was the power of dirty talk to change our partners' lives. It's no small gift to help another person feel confident and joyful about their bodies, especially sexually speaking. The second was that the two of them like to travel together, even on road trips. It takes a special someone to make road trips a pleasure instead of a terrible, prolonged experience in mounting frustration.

Chase saw a similarity in how Rosa improves both his love life and his travels using the same skills of observation and positive communication. While not all dirty talk is directly uplifting, Rosa clearly uses it that way, at least some of the time. Chase's eyes sparkled as he shared this story; it's clearly something he loves very much about her.

I had to ask Chase for more details. How did she say it, and when? Was it really right in the middle of the deed, or afterward?

"It was a while ago, but I think she more or less just blurted it out while she was . . . stroking me. She was grinning and taking me in with her eyes and her hands all at once. We were laughing together and having fun, and then she said that." He blushed and looked down, chuckling at his shyness as well as the memory.

There's a certain playfulness in his description that matches my impression of Rosa, having had lunch with her a few times. I wouldn't describe her as childlike by any means, and she has the potential to take herself entirely too seriously, but she's just as capable of contagious giggling fits over random bits of humor. When she's in a playful mood, whether sexual or platonic, she doesn't hesitate to share it with those around her.

"I spent too many years being a serious adult already," she once told me. "Sometimes you just have to laugh, and it's easier if others are laughing, too." So it's not surprising that Rosa sometimes brings the same playfulness to her dirty talk. I gave her a call to ask her for more details and perhaps a bit of inspiration, to understand how she became comfortable with playful dirty talk.

I guess it comes naturally for me, but it didn't always. I used to really worry about things being right during sex, and it was easy for me to suddenly be swept out of the mood. When that happened, sex would end badly. I would blame him for saying or doing the wrong thing, then stalk off or roll away, all frustrated and upset. I'm a real crab when I'm angry and blue-balled. Blue-clitted? Anyway, I guess I wasn't as secure then as I am now, like I treated every time as though I'd never get laid again or I hadn't in ages!

We shared a laugh, and she thought for a bit before she continued.

I guess I eventually realized a few things. First, no single time in bed should define or limit my sexual relationship with someone. Second, it gets boring, upsetting, or both if I don't laugh. I mean, face it. Bodies are funny, especially naked bodies getting it on together! If people aren't making funny faces and movements, they're making hilarious sounds. There is something special in that, though. We make ourselves all vulnerable, and that's how we really find each other as lovers. We connect because we bare a side of ourselves to our lovers that nobody else sees. It's ridiculously beautiful when you think of it like that. Even a one-night stand can really impact my life, if I connect with someone in that crazy, vulnerable, silly nakedness.

I told her about Chase's comment about their first time together, and what he remembered.

"Isn't he darling? Well, if I said it when we were getting busy, then it must be true! When I'm with Chase, those kinds of things just come out. I feel it, I notice it, or I want it then I say it. And I pretty much always want him!"

Sexual experiences should be arousing, pleasurable, playful, and routes to building deeper trust and intimacy in your relationships. The combination of erotic body language and dirty talk creates a powerful and deeply sensual source of communication, which then inspires sexual energy throughout the different facets of your life and relationships. From foreplay to sex to postcoital cuddling, dirty talk provides a fun and loving opportunity to continue to grow closer and stronger as a couple.

It's just as useful for increasing your own sexual awareness and self-esteem! While you may have started talking dirty for the fun of it, or to jump-start your relationship, why not enjoy these other benefits as well?

There's no doubt that skillful, honest, self-aware, and hedonistic communication is at the heart of the hottest dirty talk. When we're authentic about what we want, and we share that sexual joy with our partners in how we to speak with them, we continue to deepen and enhance our relationships with ourselves and our lovers. These skills can help us communicate on every level of our relationship. While it may sound cheesy, I'm a big fan of the idea of sexual healing.

Some of my colleagues in mental health and healing tend to try to fix everything except sex, trusting that the relationship's sexual component will fix itself when the rest is tended to. But I've seen many couples make amazing progress by beginning with their love lives and moving forward from there! My favorite way to work, though, is to share techniques that inspire simultaneous relational change of platonic and erotic natures. One of my favorite techniques is a simple activity I call "Awesomes and Appreciates."

I often meet women and couples whose lives are full of success and achievement, yet they remain humble as they quietly pursue the next challenge without stopping to celebrate their triumphs. I suggest that they make sure to take time to recognize the ways each of them has been amazing since we last spoke, and what they particularly appreciate about each other. It's a seemingly simple exercise that I've been doing with clients for years and years, almost as long as I've been enjoying it in my own relationship. It's also the perfect accompaniment to finding confident moments in your life that can become springboards for your dirty talk style. You can follow along with a worksheet that you'll find under the same name in Chapter 12.

Awesomes and Appreciates started at our dining room table one evening, during one of the painfully long years when my sweetie and I were both working on our doctoral degrees. We were studying very different fields; his days were full of statistical equations and mine were packed with mental health theories and practice. I felt as though we'd lost touch with each other in the process. Additionally, we couldn't always understand each other when we tried to share the nuances of our days, because our fields had us speaking completely different languages. Many couples face similar situations, whether or not they're in school. Eight or more hours spent on separate, unrelated tasks each weekday can wear on any couple's sense of unity! So we sat there, chewing our salads and eyeing our reduced-calorie entrées and mulling over our day in silence.

"I had an idea," I blurted out of nowhere, as I often do. "I feel like you're doing amazing things out there, but I don't what they are. Let's list a few things that are awesome about each of us from the day, whether it's dinky or impressive! Maybe we can do it every evening, if we like it."

We started with simple, silly statements that came most easily to our minds. When it was hard to think of something impressive, we reminded each other that little things were just as important.

I snuck a quick nap today between projects, and it felt amazing.

I had a cookie at the mixer without worrying about it, but I also didn't grab a second.

I got a paper written close enough to on time and then started the next one right away.

I just felt like I looked really sharp today.

My boss complimented me.

One of my students thanked me for helping them.

I picked up the socks I had left in the corner before you had to ask.

It was a good way to begin, and as we gained confidence we started to disclose more of our feelings along the way. We began to give ourselves permission to bask in our accomplishments a little more, and we also started sharing more personal Awesomes.

I was feeling really frightened about how behind I was with these projects, so I really knocked it out today and got back on schedule. Now I'm just giddy with confidence about being able to finish up soon and maybe get noticed for my solid work, as silly as it sounds.

I've been feeling like we're really disconnected lately. I know it's just that I miss you, but I noticed that I've been feeling crabby with you for no good reason. Instead of letting myself get cranky, I realized what was happening this afternoon and that's why I kissed you like that. I'm proud of myself for kissing you in a way you liked, and for handling it better when I miss you.

At first it was embarrassing to be the one bragging, but it also felt good somewhere deep inside. It also became fun to be the one talking as we saw how much our partner enjoyed hearing about ourselves. Soon, we added another ritual, to complement our Awesomes: Appreciates.

While Awesomes began at the dining room table, Appreciates began once we were tucked in for the night. I'd been hearing his Awesomes each day, but I wanted to do more than listen. I also felt that he'd missed a few things that belonged on his list of accomplishments.

So we began a nighttime tradition of listing a few things (nothing too comprehensive) that we appreciated about each other before bed. Even if we had been fighting moments before, we were not allowed to go to sleep without an honest set of Appreciates. Over time we moved Awesomes into the bedroom, right before Appreciates, and combined them.

Remember Lena and Dorian from Chapter 4? I clearly remember the first time they shared their Awesomes and Appreciates. Our trial run was challenging. While each was able to list an Appreciate or two, the Awesomes were even more difficult. I asked them to spend the next two weeks keeping it in mind and coming up with a list to share the next time we met. I also sent them a few reminder e-mails.

They were perplexed by how difficult it was; they're a close couple, and each is constantly glowing about the other. They're also a great team when it comes to facing challenges. The difficulty they faced shows how, when it comes to celebrating our achievements and triumphs, even the strongest couples can easily gloss over the important moments.

As I explained to them, we often get in the habit of turning to the next challenge as soon as the prior one has been conquered or goes away on its own. When a problem is fired at us, we strive to grab it, figure it out, and put it behind us as promptly as possible. It's as though we've simply tossed the achievement over our shoulder, so we can quickly focus on the next task coming our way.

After a while, we've accumulated a huge pile of achievements and successes, small and large. If we never look back to celebrate them, we'll lose track of just how impressive we are, individually and in our relationships. It's a habit that a bit of concentration and mindfulness can readily change.

The first few times were a bit more challenging for Dorian than Lena. Once Lena got a taste for celebrating accomplishments together, she was hooked. Dorian, on the other hand, was more used to quietly making life better for both of them without stopping to congratulate himself or her.

At first, he felt awkward mentioning accomplishments that happened weekly: wonderful meals made by Lena or successful tasks at work. These were the most important to share, as it turned out. Who doesn't want to know that their continued efforts are appreciated over and over again? It feels artificial at first, a sure sign that you're on the right path to breaking a stubborn habit.

Before you know it, you'll find yourself making mental notes throughout the day as you catch yourself or your sweetie being amazing. These subtle but important new habits create a path toward making your larger confident moments glow brightly in your mind! Once this transition sets in, we can use these moments to inspire us to tap into our power, whether we're working hard or enjoying the hottie across the couch.

Awesomes and Appreciates can also be used to develop playfully sexy conversation that offers helpful feedback and enhances sexual intimacy. While this isn't strictly dirty talk, it can easily turn into that, or it will at least help you gain confidence in your dirty talk efforts. According to Patricia Johnson and Mark A. Michaels in *The Essence of Tantric Sexuality*, we're especially sensitive to our lover's words right after a shared act of intimacy.

Language has a particularly strong impact on us then, a fact you can use for good instead of evil! This is not the time to critique your performance together, discuss the laundry, or bring up financial stresses. Instead, use this as an opportunity to appreciate your partner for the aspects of the seduction and pleasure that you enjoyed. But don't stop there! Include the awesome things about yourself, too!

I really appreciated the way you started with a wet touch, grabbing a bit of lube before massaging my vulva.

It got me even more turned on and helped me relax and enjoy. I felt pretty awesome for remembering to leave my favorite lube next to the bed for you, and for reminding myself to breathe and experience your touch instead of rushing to touch you right away.

If right after your lovemaking doesn't feel like the right time, then be sure to make room for it during your conversation later in the day. Don't limit it to after sex, either. Kissing, massage, or even snuggle time are perfect excuses to develop deeper emotional intimacy, connection, and understanding with this dynamic technique.

I absolutely adore it when you gently walk up behind me to hug me and kiss the back of my neck. It makes me feel so warm, protected, and sexy in the middle of an otherwise bland task. I'm so glad I asked you to do that more often so that you'd know I like it!

Now that you've become so good at Awesomes and Appreciates, you have every reason to use them to improve your love life. Be especially sure to sneak them in during your afterglow with your lover, for even more intimacy-building mileage.

Developing healthy new habits like this can take some time. Awesomes and Appreciates isn't the kind of silver bullet relationship-saving activity you're likely to see in the glossy women's magazines. There's a reason why we keep buying new issues with the same teasers on every month's cover, though: Their tricks didn't work for us the first time, and we're still looking for an effective answer! Worthwhile, lifelong individual and relationship changes should take time to develop, but they should also feel better and better as you continue to practice them.

I see sexual well-being and confidence in much the same way. While there's strong merit in the "fake it till you make it" approach to sexual confidence and dirty talk, and it can create lasting change, it's often stressful and unpleasant during the fake-it period. Replacing a troublesome habit with a desirable new pattern usually starts with a jolting initial change as we identify the problem spots and push ourselves in the new direction.

It's less likely to last if we don't feel an authentic sense of motivation, worth, and inspiration behind the effort to change. If you don't feel that you honestly deserve a healthier body, and you take no pleasure in working out, your new exercise routine won't stick past the next bakery. But if you treat your trips to the gym with the same level of entitlement and joy as a spa pedicure date, it's more likely to get you to your goals. Allowing your sexual confidence and feminine power to glow isn't pompous or off-putting when it encourages others to smile and celebrate their own sexiness with you.

This is a radically new approach to celebrating our eroticism with our partners, especially for certain generations of women who have pored over books, articles, and salon conversations on how to please (and thus keep) a man. Regardless of the gender of your sweetie, if you're a woman, then taking responsibility for your partner's sexual satisfaction is as encouraged as taking responsibility for keeping everyone fed and for scheduling the family's dental appointments.

In exchange, we hope that our male partners will be that sexual knight in shining armor who's come to sweep us off our feet and into pleasure. If he isn't, we wish he'd change, but we also don't want to make him feel bad about it. Better to accept the situation or look for delicate avenues for help with getting him to live up to that expectation.

Sex is a delicate matter, and we don't want to traumatize the poor guy and make him distant. Meanwhile, we continue to try to live up to our sexual obligations until we just can't take it anymore, at which point we may hire a professional to try to fix us. And the cycle repeats.

For women who find themselves in a pattern like this, it may feel dramatically counterintuitive to start with confidence and self-aware entitlement. Yet these traits can inspire unmatched erotic energy and breathtaking sex! A woman who's tapped into her sexual and feminine power enjoys discovering what gives her pleasure and relishes in the shared pleasure of eliciting it from her lovers.

With worries and insecurities out the way, at least for the moment, sexual expression can become a natural and authentic aspect of flirting and lovemaking. When dirty talk comes this naturally, there's no need to resort to ill-fitting and stifling sexual stereotypes. Your own personality, whichever facet feels right in the moment, becomes the basis for your dirty talk style. You become a goddess of delight, just as you are, and who could resist?

Key Points

- Dirty talk provides an essential outlet for grown-up, sexual play with our partners.
- It's also a powerful way to build emotional and sexual intimacy through better communication skills that can overlap into every area of your relationship.
- Dirty talk need not end after intercourse. Use the time after you've been intimate to share your favorite parts of the experience and lift each other up.

EXERCISE

Turn to Chapter 12 to explore your Awesomes and Appreciates. This is a useful technique for building your relationship both erotically and nonsexually. See if you can use it to appreciate sexual and nonsexual things about yourself and your partner each night, making it a regular ritual as a couple.

TWELVE

Inspiring Exercises

Find Your Confident Moment

Step 1: Center yourself, wherever you are.

If you can close your eyes for a bit, do so. Otherwise, allow yourself to tune out the world around you. Sink into your chair and take a moment to feel your feet on the floor, your hips on your chair, and the air on your skin. If you cannot quite let go, grab a pen and jot down the main thoughts buzzing through your mind, so you can let go and return to them later without forgetting. Enjoy quietness in your body and mind for a moment, even if your surroundings are anything but calm. Breathe in deeply through your nose, feel your lungs fill, and exhale out your mouth. Imagine yourself as a peaceful, healthy, and private island.

Step 2: Focus on a confident memory.

Somewhere, at some point, you felt really darned good about yourself and confident in something you had done, felt, said, or experienced. It may not be a story you think about often, and perhaps you've never even shared it. Or it may be your favorite anecdote to tell at parties. Either is fine! While you're centered and calm, remember as many details as you can about that moment. Pick up a pen and paper, or something to type with, and make notes for yourself.

Step 3: Expand on the details.

Who were you with? What kind of title, position, role, or job did you have in that situation? When did this happen? How did you prepare for this moment, if you did? What was or is special about you that allowed this to happen? Who witnessed this moment, or who do you wish had witnessed it with you? How did people respond when they heard, or how do you imagine they might respond?

Step 4: What does this reveal about you?

The moments we remember, and the details we recall about them, are deeply symbolic of who we are and who we can become. You can use these confident moments to reconceptualize your story or yourself as a sexual being. Your past is likely to be filled with many such moments that don't necessarily make it into the final cut of your own narrative of your identity and history. You can use them to change how you think about yourself by letting them inspire you to channel your sexual energy and self-confidence more often!

Dirty Talk Style Guide

Create your own dirty talk description using elements from Ellie's, Rochelle's, and Marny's stories and adjusting them to match you. It's not necessarily best to answer these questions in order—read through them and answer the questions as they catch your interest. Your answers may be sentences, phrases, or a list of words that come to mind.

My style's name: _____

I am most confident when: _____

_____

I am (or would be) most turned on when I am: _____

_____

_____

I am (or would be) most turned on when my partner is:

_____

_____

My flirtatious or dirty talk style can best be described as:

_____

_____

*I imagine that other women with a similar style would look
and act like:* _____

_____

*I would like to be able to tell my partner these things about
my sexual side:* _____

_____

I would like my partner to respond by: _____

_____

*I would be happiest and most turned on if the mood of my
dirty talk were:* _____

_____

Sensual Item Guide

Pick a time when you're feeling relaxed, confident, and sensual. Move to your bedroom and allow yourself to browse, hold, and smell various wearable items that draw your attention. Allow yourself to gravitate to one item that you could wear, decorate, or accessorize yourself with and that makes you feel particularly confident and erotic. What does this item tell you about yourself and the dirty talking style and character that appeals to you? Take your time listing words, phrases, or full answers to each question.

How does your item feel, smell, sound, or taste?

_____

_____

What visual aspects of this item draw your attention the most? _____

_____

If this item were worn (or held) at a suitable event, what would it say about you to those who saw you?

_____

_____

What attracted you to this item when you first found it or received it? _____

_____

How does this item make you feel about yourself when you wear, hold, or use it? _____

_____

What kind of woman could flaunt this item in just the right way? _____

_____

Once you've answered each question, reread what you've written. This time, allow the item to represent an erotic character stemming from a facet of yourself. Apply each answer to yourself, and use these answers to describe who you can be as a seductive dirty talker.

Sensual Language Guide

Choose a sensual drink, dessert, berry, or piece of fruit that you enjoy and turn it into a delicious excuse to build your dirty talk vocabulary through sensual language skills!

Step 1

Before eating your treat, take a moment to relax and clear your mind. Ensure that you have at least half an hour of uninterrupted time for this activity, if not an hour. Turn off your computer and your cell phone. Yes, turn them all the way off so no portion of your mind is left wondering if they'll buzz or ding. Concentrate on picturing the treat in your mind, and imagine going through the steps of bringing it to your table using slow, mindful motions. Then you may go get your treat, being careful not to rush so that you can absorb the act through every sense.

Step 2

Don't bother to use utensils. Place a napkin under the treat or tuck it into a towel if it may be messy, as you'll be eating with your fingers. Slowly explore your treat through all five senses. I suggest using this order: sight, touch, smell, sound, taste. Some senses will overlap if you do a good job.

Step 3

Every few moments stop to write your sensual, descriptive words and phrases using a pen and paper. Don't type them unless you absolutely must, as handwriting is more expressive and personal. Strive for at least ten words and phrases for each sense. If you're struggling to find that many, slow down and relax into the experience and let the treat guide and seduce you.

Step 4

After you're done and you've cleaned up, take your pen and paper to another room and spend some time remembering the experience. Revisit your written list and flesh it out. As you're able, turn your words into more detailed phrases and sentences. If you need more inspiration, repeat the above steps with various treats until the exercise feels natural and enjoyable, and words flow freely for you.

Fantasies for the Shy

I'm in on your little secret: You're not quite as shy as you think you are! In fact, you've got a fantasy just waiting to materialize. Use this guide to help you put together the perfect elements for your own night, day, or weekend of fantasy-fueled passion and intimacy. Don't worry about pleasing anyone other than yourself right now. This is all about you and your fantasies!

The Plot
What is the story line of your fantasy? _____

_____

_____

_____

_____

_____

The Mood
What tone or personality do you want to base your fantasy on? _____

_____

_____

_____

_____

_____

The Words and Sensations

What words or feelings are essential to your arousal in this fantasy? _____

_____

_____

_____

_____

The Pleasure

How will your fantasy culminate? What act of pleasure are you hoping to experience? _____

_____

_____

_____

_____

Awesomes and Appreciates

Step 1: Awesomes

Begin by listing things about yourself that make you (or at least could make you) feel proud. These may be small accomplishments, natural aspects of your personality shining through, or major achievements. Nothing is too small or too big; everything counts. At the same time, this need not be an exhaustive list. I suggest aiming for three to ten items, but use your judgment. You have permission to brag and be proud during this activity, so make the most of it!

List your Awesomes all at once, instead of going back and forth between you and your partner. The listening partner should keep any comments brief and affirmatively curious. It's appropriate to ask for more details to help the other person reveal and relive how awesome they are, and to make quick comments of direct support. Never question whether something is actually Awesome, share a one-up, or share your own stories while you're listening. This is the speaker's time to shine; your job is to help your partner glow more strongly.

Step 2: Appreciates

After everyone involved has shared their Awesomes and affirmed each other, it's time to share Appreciates. Strive to list about three to ten things that you admired or found meaningful about your partner in the recent past. Again, nothing is too big, too small, or too mundane. In fact, it's especially important to appreciate the things we do for each other day after day, lest they be taken for granted. You may list some things that your partner gave as Awesomes, but don't feel pressured to list all of them.

If you're listening, don't be downhearted if something that mattered to you didn't make your partner's list. Instead, focus on receiving their appreciation and reveling in it. It's appropriate to ask brief questions to clarify the appreciation, but never to question the value of what the other has listed. If you find yourself wishing your partner had listed things they didn't, you may wish to start offering Appreciates before Awesomes, so you can make sure those things are included during the second half of this activity.

Step 3: Warm, Fuzzy Feelings

This activity isn't over when the speaking is done. Now it's time to deeply feel what an amazing team you can be together. Spend a few moments being physically close, whether it's hugging, making love, holding hands, or snuggling before falling asleep. Instead of using words, let your body language do the talking at the end of this activity.

THIRTEEN

Sample Scripts

Throughout this book you've read many examples of dirty talk and heard from numerous couples and individuals about their thoughts on the topic. I also invited my friends, clients, and online connections to share their own dirty talk scripts with you. These are all real-life examples of real people talking dirty, from kinky singles to committed couples to professional sex workers. Let their voices inspire your own!

Excerpts from Jenny's Sensual Description of Fruit Salad

I opened the refrigerator door and thought, "Oh, I'd like to have that." As I rinsed the berries, the water washed over the fruit, making the skin shiny and wet. I realized that it was as though I was giving the fruit a shower. One of the berries was calling to me, so I picked it up. It was plump, firm, and I was filled with anticipation because it was going to taste delicious. The color was bright and deep, calling me to eat it first. The texture of the fruit's skin looked smooth and I wanted to feel it in my mouth. It was the exact right ripeness, letting me know that it was ready for me. I knew there would be a ripe, burst of flavor that would come from biting into it and I thought, "This is going to be juicy!"

The perfect berry feels just right in my fingers. It is firm, yet inside there is the right softness. The texture matches what I'm looking for: firm and rough, yet smooth. When fruit is ready to be eaten, it wants you to know, just like how lovers' bodies display their readiness for each other. Tasting the fruit brought a rush of sensations as I was touching it with my mouth. The taste of the skin and flavors of the juice combined, and I could feel the firmness at the same time that I was tasting the sweet, tart juices. The scent of the fruit was pungent and sweet at the same time. Various parts smelled differently, and once it had been tasted it smelled as though it wanted to be tasted again. Each berry had a distinct flavor. The blackberries were mild and less intense, offering a soft break between the more intense berries with their mellow, smooth, and delicate taste. The strawberries were tart and sweet at the same time, and offered the most juice while the tartness made me salivate. I could feel the juice as it spread in my mouth; I felt it on my tongue but it gave the impression that I could feel it everywhere in my mouth and not just on the tongue. The blueberries, on the other hand, were like an intoxicating, dry wine.

Favorite Dirty Talk Quotes

When I asked for short dirty talk narratives on my blog and through Twitter, I was flooded with submissions! Here are three of my favorite quickies:

The most seductive word I've ever heard is "yes" spoken slowly, rolling off the lips of my lover in a near-whisper. —Anonymous

I'll give you whatever you want but if you want it, if you want me, you're going to have to ask for it. —Anonymous

I love you, I miss you, I can still taste you on my tongue . . . spending time with you is so good, so easy. Thank you, my love. —Kyle to Roxyr

Text Messages, Phone Conversations, E-mails, and Voice Mails

My friend Electra_4 wanted to share a text message exchange that quickly led to some steamy phone sex with her partner!

Me: I wanna do bad things to you . . . but, alas, I must write essays.

Partner: Still have my marks on you?

M: Sadly, no . . . You'll just have to give me some new ones. I do so miss being marked. I can still feel where I was bitten, if I press down, but nothing visible . . .

M: Damn you . . . now I can't get my mind out of the gutter.

P: Well, don't think about having your hands tied behind you, my hand on your throat, teeth sinking into your tender flesh.

P: Because that wouldn't help at all . . .

M: Oh fuck you . . . you're not helping.

P: It's not my fault you're a dirty slut.

M: Mmmm . . . but being a slut is so much fun . . . sucking your cock as you stand over me, trying to make you cum in my mouth, on my face . . . or being bent down onto my knees, bent over and fucked like a bitch . . . how could any girl not like that.

(And then there was much dialing of phone numbers, less texting, and no completing of essays.)

The following are text message exchanges between Jo Whole and her partner, Peter. Both of them are adults, but they enjoy fantasizing and role-playing together with Peter as a sexy daddy and Jo as his little girl.

Peter: How's my little girl?

Jo: I'm good. Stressed, but good. You know, work and stuff.

P: Ah, well, you don't have to worry about that when you're with me. Just come and sit on my lap. Have a cuddle.

J: You're already making my pussy tingle!

P: Are you all smooth?

J: I will be for you by tomorrow night.

P: Good girl. I'll let you come and slip into my bed. Snuggle against me.

J: And be cared for. Can I bounce up and down on your cock, Daddy? Like a bouncy castle?

P: Naughty girl. If you are good and do what you are told. Share with Daddy.

J: Thank you, Daddy. I will certainly do as I am told.

P: Trust Daddy, let him teach you.

J: What are you going to teach me?

P: How to be a big girl.

J: I thought I was pretty good at being a big girl already.

P: You will have to look after your Daddy.

J: I would love to look after my Daddy!

P: Good girl. How will you look after your Daddy?

J: I can look after my Daddy for as much time as he will let me! It would be kinda hot to be "kept" naked and waiting.

P: Keeping you naked is kind of hot. I could take your clothes. Confiscate them, keep you there. My special girl. Would you like that?

J: I would love that!

P: If you wanted clothes, you would have to wear Daddy's. His T-shirt, but nothing on bottom. Open, wet, inviting. Let Daddy rub your back, pat your bottom.

J: Could it be a button-down shirt of yours? That would be sexy.

P: Yes. Are there new things you have been thinking of that we will do? That I will do to you? In addition to me touching you, filling you, your ass. You licking my ass. Keeping you naked, open. Mine.

J: Yours. Open, wet. How about you and me with Jenny in the bathroom of a bar? You fingering her ass from behind while I finger her pussy from in front, sandwiching her.

P: Mmm, very hot. Send you and Jenny to the ladies room while we are having dinner at a nice restaurant.

J: Mmm, and I lick her until she comes? Can't come back to the table until she does?

P: Yes! Not allowed to clean up after. Bring her panties back to me.

J: And then all my food will taste like yummy pussy. Is her pussy tasty, Daddy?

P: Yes, not strong, but nice.

J: Does she like having her ass fingered while being licked?

P: Oh, yes, and fucked from behind. Fingers in ass as being fucked.

J: I miss the feel of your cock deep in my ass, balls-deep, pounding away.

P: I only fucked her ass for the first time in November. She practiced. She took it all, deep.

J: Oh, wow. Well, you're big. We can DP her too. Can we both fit in her pussy? I love having two cocks in my pussy, getting off on rubbing each other.

P: I like that, seeing you suck two cocks at once—mine one of them. Having you both suck my cock.

J: I'd also like to be cuckolded with you giving all your attention and caring to Jenny while I'm somehow left out, restrained, or ignored.

P: Kept in the corner, chastity belt, unable to touch.

J: Yes, Daddy.

P: *Seeing me pound, smack, fuck, come. No come for little girl if she has been bad.*

(Jo pouts.)

P: *You can only have what you get secondhand from Jenny. Lick it from Jenny's pussy or ass.*

J: *Come-licking and swapping.*

P: *A very hot thought. I just came. Oh, my.*

J: *Guess you liked that idea! (She smiles.)*

P: *Very hot. Wow.*

J: *Yay, I made Daddy come hard.*

P: *You did.*

J: *If you want to help me go to sleep, can you tell me sexy things to jerk off to?*

P: *Okay. My hand . . . stroking your hair, your neck. Whispering to you. Knowing how special you are, how good you are. Mine, open, dirty, depraved. Special.*

J: *I'm working toward being fistable for you.*

P: *Beautiful. For me? You are beautiful.*

J: *Thank you! I have very warm, fuzzy feelings for you.*

P: *Wet feelings?*

J: *Very wet.*

P: *Dribbling down your ass crack?*

J: *Not right now, but that would be yummy.*

P: *Taste it.*

J: Yes, Daddy. Tastes orangey because I've been peeling and eating clementines.

P: Oh, my, you are beautiful. But for now, you must sleep. Be calm, think of warm thoughts.

J: Without coming?

P: When your computer is off. Nothing but you and me.

J: I can come when the computer is off?

P: Yes. Turn it all off. Be naked, be mine. Come for me.

J: Yes, Daddy, I will. I won't come until we say good night. I will focus on you alone.

P: Thank you. Yes. E-mail me in the morning after a deep sleep.

J: Yes, Daddy. Night night.

P: Night night. I will wake to your e-mail. (Peter gives her a wet kiss and touches her bottom.) Mine.

J: Yes, Daddy. Yours. Yours, yours, yours.

P: Thinking of wrapping my arms around you, snuggling in close, stroking your hair. Light kisses on head. Pulling you down onto my hard cock.

J: Oh, wow. Your gorgeous cock.

P: Pushing, choking, filling. Fingers deep in your ass, touching.

J: I want to do a good job for Daddy, being open.

P: Yes, fill you. Penetrate you. Open you. Be inside you.

J: *Our connection when we're intertwined like that is amazing. Tight, squeezing your fingers and cock, moaning into you.*

P: *Mmm. Stretching you, pushing you, rotating inside you. Your cunt stretched around my wrist. My dirty girl.*

J: *I want to be open for you like that.*

P: *My ass licker.*

J: *Yes, I love licking your ass.*

P: *Pushing, slapping your face with my cock.*

J: *So intense, trusting you like that.*

P: *Yes. Trusting me to choose. Having my balls in your mouth, cock against your face.*

J: *Whatever you want in my mouth is in my mouth.*

P: *Cheeky girl.*

J: *Yup. Cheeky. That's me.*

(Peter pats her on the bottom.)

P: *Daddy is horny.*

J: *I'd love to gobble your cock up for you.*

P: *Mmm. Force it in deep, slap your face with it, sit on your face with my balls in your mouth.*

J: *Mmm, you are so sweet, daddy.*

P: *You are a special girl, dirty girl. Take your pants off?*

J: *Sure. Will do.*

P: *Good girl. And panties.*

J: *Shirt too?*

P: *No. Half undressed, exposed, nice.*

J: *Yes, Daddy.*

P: *Are you smooth?*

J: *No, I only shave when I have reason to.*

P: *Just for porn?*

J: *Or Daddy.*

P: *Yay, yes. Always for Daddy.*

J: *Do you want me to shave for you right now?*

P: *Oh, my, yes, but when we have finished. Good girl.*

J: *Do you need me to stay shaved even while we're apart?*

P: *Yes, mine. My cunt, smooth cunt. Would you do that for me? To remember, all the time?*

J: *I don't want to, but I would for you, Daddy, if I have to. I will shave for you tonight, Daddy. Be all smooth while I play with myself.*

P: *Thank you. (He strokes her hair.) Little girls who play might get spanked. Have you been having naughty thoughts? Tell me. I like thinking of how naughty you are.*

J: *Is Daddy hard and stroking?*

P: *I am. You are very hot.*

J: *Thank you, Daddy.*

P: Is your cunt wet? Check, touch. Taste. Rub on your cunt, ass, for me. Imagine me there doing it, making you do it.

J: Fingers only or can I use vibrator?

P: Fingers for now.

J: Yes, Daddy. Hard to type, though.

P: Mmm, just imagining. I will let you finish now as you're about to go and shave for your Daddy.

J: Finish? With my vibe?

P: Stop touching.

(Jo pouts.)

P: After you shave, little girl.

(Jo sulks.)

J: Yes, Daddy.

(Peter smacks Jo on the bottom.)

J: Thank you, Daddy.

P: I am just stressed and tired.

J: So what you're saying is that you really need your cock sucked to relax you? (smiles)

P (laughs): Yes, I suppose so.

J: I really do wish I could contribute to your relaxation, not your stress.

P: Thank you. You are kind.

J: I care. And you work very hard. If I were chained up in your bedroom closet in a way that you didn't have to think about or worry about me at all until that exact moment right before bed when you wanted to use my mouth, pussy, and/or ass to get yourself off, that would be delightful.

P: That is a beautiful thought. Say more.

J: I wouldn't want to be there in a way that would contribute to your stress. If I could just be a little stress relief valve for you, that would be good. I would feel useful.

P: Kept in the closet, used.

J: Be your fuck toy. Used to get you off and then put back away, even if I'm still horny or want more, just there to service you and your needs.

P: You are such a good girl. Caring girl, giving girl.

J: Thank you, Daddy.

P: How could I use you? How would you service me?

J: In whatever way suits you best. If you just want to get off, pick a hole and use it to dump your come in. If you want to savor it, tell me exactly how you want to be serviced and I will comply. If you're tired, tell me to do all the work and get on top and ride you or work your cock over with my magic hands. If you're in the mood to hurt me, that's of course your prerogative.

P: Tell me how I may hurt you, how you like to be hurt.

J: Well, it wouldn't have to be limited to how I like to be hurt. I'd want you to hurt me for you, not for me, and I would take it for you gladly as a way to help you recover from your stressful day.

P: Cane you? Your bottom?

J: Yes, please, Daddy, however makes you happy.

P: Thank you, little girl. Thank you for cheering me up.

Dr. Susana Mayer is the founder of the Erotic Literary Salon in Philadelphia, Pennsylvania (www.TheEroticLiterarySalon .com), and is writing her first book on erotica. She submitted these steamy e-mail exchanges with Jay.

E-mail 1

Susana: Excuse me, but why was I not informed of your fantasy? I would love to sit on your rod and have a slow steamy fuck, while your hands squeeze my ass, stretch my hole, tip of your cock playing with my rim, fuck in slow motion, coming all the way out then deep to the inner folds, fingertips playing with rim as the rod pumps deep, glides in wet and changes pace to tease the shit out of me and your cock.

Jay: God, I feel me inside you already. You expect me teach today with that image in my mind? You must be crazy. I will lick that wonderful, curvy ass, kiss it, caress it, finger it, eat it, fuck it. Damn, I am hard now!

E-mail 2

Susana: I would love to be sucking on you right now. I have a jones for your cock. You're squirming while reading, hopefully no one looking over your shoulder. Never had such a strong feeling without you in my presence. And so I shall in my thoughts, tongue your rim, lick your tip, and suck you dry while fondling your magnificent balls. I do love pleasuring you and being pleasured by this act. I will lay my head on your fuzz while you play with the tendrils of my hair and we doze off to a wondrous slumber, holding tight as we pleasure each other in our dreams.

E-mail 3

Jay: I love the intensity of our coupling. It feels so good to me, and I am glad to see you enjoy it. I sometimes get somewhat guilty because I know how incredible it is for me, and I want you to know some of that exquisite joy too. When you pleasured yourself when I was lying next to you—that felt so special, so joined. Never had that experience before. With you, it all seems so right. Thank you. I love you.

Susana: Wow! An experience you never had before, a woman pleasuring herself lying in your arms. I know you tell the truth, yet I find it hard to believe. I guess I have not done that before with you—are you sure? Someday I would love to reverse roles, have you ever pleasured yourself in the arms of a woman?

Guilty, for what? Can you not feel the ecstasy oozing out of every pore? My body twitching, shaking on edge, my breathing, my sounds, my "no" sound moments. Guilty, are you joking? Sweetheart, you are an incredible lover. Lying in your arms, pleasuring myself was my body being selfish wanting more. I had had so many orgasms while you were inside me, and yet, snuggling with you, feeling your softness between my crack just turned me on all over again, totally selfish. My clit was crying out to be touched, and these days it takes forever. I truly didn't think I would orgasm, hadn't planned on it, just wanted to enjoy my touch, entwined in your arms. I came, rather quickly for me, and so intense.

My insides felt totally exposed. And as I write this the feelings are there again. I shall pleasure myself with a vibrator. Damn, what you do to me.

Jay: I am smiling, and the hard-on is there. What you do to me! No, that was a first for me. People have masturbated in front of me, but not while we were snuggled. It was so erotic, so close, so personal. I loved it. And I do love hearing and seeing your pleasure. We share and give and receive pleasure so openly and thoroughly. That is so special. Have a great day—I love you.

Susana: Good morning dearest. Kisses, perhaps a hard-on to start your day.

Cameryn Moore (www.camerynmoore.com) is a phone sex operator and the performance artist responsible for the amazing one-woman play *Phone Whore*. She was kind enough to share an example of one of her real-life calls, from a gentleman who wanted to be the best pussy-eater she had ever had.

Cameryn: Hi, Eric, it's Cameryn.

Eric: Hi, Cameryn.

C: How are you doing tonight?

E: Pretty good.

C: Yeah? I bet we can turn that into really, really great before we finish. What do you think?

E: I hope so.

C: Well, I'll do my best. I don't think we've spoken before. Do you want to hear a little about me, or do you want to tell me about yourself first?

E: Tell me about you.

C: Okay. Well, I'm forty-four years old. I'm a tall girl, five feet nine inches. I've got [size] forty-two DDD tits . . .

E: Wow.

C: I certainly don't get any complaints! Let's see . . . I have a nice round ass to match, so I'm a little bit of an hourglass.

E: Mmmm.

C: Ha ha, I can tell what you'd be looking at if I walked into your room right now! . . . I've got long legs. Short, wavy, dark blonde hair, and blue eyes. And I've been around the block a little bit, so anything you want to throw at me, I can catch it and run with it.

E: You sound amazing.

C: Well, I have a good time . . . So. You like the look of my ass, huh?

E: Oh, yeah.

C: Or is it my pussy you want?

E: Your pussy. I would love to eat that all night.

C: So you say. But I want to know how hungry you are. I'm gonna walk in the room and sit down on a chair across from you, my long legs open wide and my skirt riding up slightly above my knees. You're looking, aren't you . . .

E: Yes.

C: I know you want a look up my skirt. The way you're sitting there on the edge of the chair and shaking. You can practically see the heat rising from me. I raise my *skirt higher and slide down lower in the easy chair. See it?*

E: Are you hairy?

C: Yes, baby. Can't you see it? The curly dark-blonde hair, the deep pink lips, the pale skin of my tender inner thighs. You can almost smell it, if you could just get closer. You want to get closer?

E: Please!

C: Well, get down here between my legs. Ah-ah-aah. Stop here. I slide my palm down your cheek, and then run my fingers through your hair to the back of your head and slowly bring you forward to about six or eight inches away from my pussy. I want you to watch, but not taste, just yet. I want you to be desperate. Are you desperate?

E: Yes!

C: No, you're not. You just sit there and watch my right hand while it trails up my inner thigh. I slowly inch my hand up until my index finger is resting just above my clit. I press my finger down and pull up hard, so that my pink lips are stretched up, long and tight. When I release my finger, the lips relax back down into soft velvet folds. You can smell me, warm and musky. Smells good, doesn't it?

E: Oh yeah, oh yeah.

C: I'm gonna reach my finger down further and trace my labia, up one side and down the other, just running my fingertip along the edges and tugging slightly so you can see the darker inner folds, slick with my juice. You're getting thirsty now too, aren't you?

E: Yesss . . .

C: You wanna taste it?

E: Yeah, oh, yeah.

C: I'm gonna dip my fingers in my pussy, two fingers, and draw them out, sticky wet. Tilt your head back and open your mouth, baby.

E: Mmmmm . . .

C :That's right. You're going to suck it all clean, between my fingers, the edges of my nails. Tastes so good, doesn't it?

E: Mmm HMMMM.

C: You want some more?

E: Yeah, yeah, please, yeah.

C: Please what.

E: Please can I eat your pussy?

C: I have to check something first. I'm going to lean forward and squeeze that cock. Ooh, that's really hard. You're just about ready to pop, huh?

E: Yessss! Oh my god, oh my god, oh my god.

C: Here, I'm going to slide my hips back down to the edge of the chair, my knees flung wide and my pussy spread open, and then pull your head forward. Get in there, baby. Show me how hungry you are. Oh, yeah, nibble and kiss up and down each side, and then bring your lips together right over my clit and give that a nice hard suck.

E: Come in my mouth, come in my mouth, please!

C: You want me to squirt? Then you better get two fingers up in my cunt and find that spot on the roof of my pussy, you know where it is. Work it, baby, work it good. That's right, THAT'S RIGHT, OH MY GOD, YES YES YES YES, OH MY GOD, OH MY GOD, OH GOD OH GOD OH GOD OH GOD DON'T YOU STOP . . . and the wetness spurts out in two or three splashes across your mouth and chin. Don't stop. Don't you dare stop. Drink it up. Drink it all up.

(He comes.)

Mmmmm . . . So. You still only good, or did we get you up to awesome?

Cameryn takes calls from men with interests that are more diverse than you or I can imagine! Often a little dirty talk with her allows them to share what they're really hoping for when they're too shy to ask.

C: Hi, Jason, it's Cameryn.

J: Hey there, Cameryn.

C: How are you doing today?

J: I'm really horny.

C: (laughs) Well, good. I think we can do something about that.

J: I hope so, I've been stroking myself for an hour, and I am so ready to come.

C: I can tell! So, have you been watching any porn while you're stroking that hard cock?

J: Oh, yeah. I'm at <name of porn star>'s web site. You ever see her stuff?

C: I know the name, but it's been a while. What's she doing right now?

J: Oh, she's on her knees sucking this guy's cock.

C: What, like deep-throating?

J: She's trying.

C: But it's too big?

J: Yeah, it's about the size of mine.

C: You can't say something like that and not tell me exact measurements.

J: It's a little over nine inches.

C: Really.

J: Yep.

C: I'm guessing you have a lot of problems finding someone who can take that all the way.

J: Yeah.

C: Well, Jason, you definitely picked the right girl today. I'm so hungry for some cock, and I can deep-throat up to ten inches.

J: Really?

C: Oh, yes. So you're not going to hold back on me, are you?

J: Hell, no.

C: *Let me get down there and get that all slicked up. First I'm going to gently brush your ball sac with my fingertips, so smooth and light. Does that feel good?*

J: *Ohhh... you makin' me shiver, baby.*

C: *Mmmm. Maybe get my lips under there and just lick and kiss you all around on your balls. (slurping noises) Mmmm, god. I can feel your cock getting all heavy and hard against my cheek.*

J: *Oh, yeah.*

C: *Yeah? (BEAT) Mmmm. I love how you smell down there. And when your balls get all tight like that, I know you're going to give me a really big load at the end, aren't you?*

J: *So fucking big.*

C: *Mmmm. (more slurping noise) Let me bathe your balls with my tongue, one at a time, so warm and velvety wet. Do you have precum already? Cuz I want to taste it. (BEAT) Oh, yeah. Just stick my tongue out and pick up that clear little drop, mmmm, tastes so good!*

J: *I'm gonna give you a lot more than that in a little bit.*

C: *I bet you are. Now I'm slipping the head of your cock in my mouth, I'm just gonna fasten my lips around the head and suck gently. My tongue is probing your pee-hole. Ooh, you like that, don't you? And that spot down there on the underside, gonna flick that with my tongue, make you jump. While I'm doing that, I'm gonna make a tight little circle out of my thumb and forefinger, and wrap that around the base of your thick shaft. I wanna feel the pulse right there at the base. I bet your cock is really throbbing, isn't it, Jason?*

J: Yesss... Jeezus. Get under there.

C: Under where?

J: Back behind my balls, bitch! Lick it.

C: Oh, you like that spot, huh? You dirty bastard. Spread your legs a little wider, if you want me to lick your ass.

J: Do it, yeah.

C: Tell you what, baby. Why don't I lie down on my back, and you can straddle my face. Just sit that sweet ass right down here.

J: Oh yeah. Dig that tongue in.

C: (Moaning and slurping noises) Mmmph, yes! I got one hand holding your ass cheeks open, and the other one is wrapped around that big thick cock. That's right, keep riding my face, let me swipe my tongue all the way from the top of your ass crack to the back of your balls. Get my makeup all fucked up, I don't care, I just wanna stick my tongue in there as deep as I can. You like a finger up in there?

J: Yeah, one of my exes did it once, I liked it...

C: Well, then lift your ass a little from my face, and let me just start tracing around your asshole with my fingertip. Hmmm. I can tell you like it, that pretty little hole is winking at me.

J: Oh, god, oh, god, yes. Don't stop...

C: Oh, I won't. I'm just gonna slide the tip of my finger in, really careful and slow, and with my other hand I'm still stroking your cock, long hard strokes.

J: *Oh god, oh, god....*

C: *You want it deeper, baby?*

J: *Just a little, oh, god, oh, god.*

C: *That's right, feel that friction while I'm sliding my finger in there, just a little twitch when I curve it up inside of that tight little asshole, I can feel how much you like that, your cock is getting so hard in my hand, and your hole is clamping down hard, jeezus Christ, so fucking tight.*

J: *Oh, shit! (comes hard)*

C: *Oh, yes, give it to me baby, I'm gonna aim that all over my pussy, splatter me with it, yes! Whew!*

J: *Mmm, damn, that was good.*

C: *(mock-scolding him) Well, next time you tell me what you really want first thing, all right? Don't have me knocking on the front door, if you want me to come in from the back!*

Resources

Sex-Positive Professionals Listings

AASECT International: www.aasect.org/directory.asp
Kink Aware Professionals (from the National Coalition for
    Sexual Freedom): www.ncsfreedom.org/kap.html
Society for Sex Therapy and Research (sex therapist
    directory): www.sstarnet.org/directory.cfm

Sexual Well-Being Authors and Professionals

Dr. Ruth Neustifter: www.exploringintimacy.com
Megan Andelloux (founder of the Center for Sexual Pleasure
    and Health): ohmegan.com
Buck Angel (media figure and educator):
    buckangelentertainment.com
Marcia Baczynski (educator, author, and consultant;
    cocreator of Cuddle Parties):
    www.askingforwhatyouwant.com
Susie Bright (prolific writer, activist, and educator):
    susiebright.blogs.com
Barbara Carrellas (educator, author, artist, and tantra
    expert): barbaracarrellas.com
Heather Corinna (activist, educator, photographer, and
    author): www.heathercorinna.com

Betty Dodson (renowned women's masturbation expert): dodsonandross.com

Amy Jo Goddard (sexuality educator, women's sexual empowerment): amyjogoddard.com

Lee Harrington (educator, author, artist, and shaman): passionandsoul.com

Nina Hartley (pornographer, author, and educator): www.nina.com

Dr. Debby Herbenick (sexuality educator and author): www.mysexprofessor.com

Patricia Johnson and Mark A. Michaels (married tantra educators and authors): www.tantrapm.com

Petra Joy (porn from a feminist perspective): www.petrajoy.com

Shanna Katz (media figure and educator): shannakatz.com

Erika Lust (filmmaker and journalist): www.erikalust.com

Reid Mihalko (educator; cocreator of Cuddle Parties): reidaboutsex.com

Cameryn Moore (performance artist): www.camerynmoore.com

Joan Price (sex and aging educator and author): www.joanprice.com

Carol Queen (renowned author, educator, and artist): www.carolqueen.com

Audacia Ray (media maker and advocate): audaciaray.com

Wrenna Robertson (editor of the photo book *I'll Show You Mine*): www.showoffbooks.com

Annie Sprinkle (renowned artist, sexologist, and author): anniesprinkle.org

Tristan Taormino (female sexuality author, educator, and pornographer): www.puckerup.com

Anita Wagner (polyamory expert and educator): www.practicalpolyamory.com

Dr. Richard Wagner (clinical sexologist and podcaster):
www.drdicksexadvice.com

Dr. Ruth Westheimer (renowned sexuality expert):
drruth.com

Additional Sexual Well-Being Resources

Cory Silverberg's About Sexuality Guide:
sexuality.about.com

Go Ask Alice (Columbia University's health Q&A Internet
service): www.goaskalice.columbia.edu

Passionate U (on-demand erotic education videos by
excellent educators): www.kinkacademy.com

San Francisco Sex Information: sfsi.org

Scarleteen (a young adult sex-ed resource filled with useful
info for all ages): www.Scarleteen.com

Society of Obstetricians and Gynaecologists of Canada
sexual health information: sexualityandu.ca

Other Amorata Press Books

101 Sex Positions: Steamy New Positions from Mild to Wild
Samantha Taylor, $17.95
This sensually illustrated book guides lovers from the straightforward to the adventurous while emphasizing the fun and enjoyment of experimenting with previously unexplored pleasures.

365 Sex Positions: A New Way Every Day for a Steamy, Erotic Year
Lisa Sweet, $17.95
With provocative photos and a belief that nothing heats up a couple's bedroom as fast as a new position, this book is the ultimate tool for achieving higher levels of pleasure.

Female Ejaculation: Unleash the Ultimate G-Spot Orgasm
Somraj Pokras and Jeffre TallTrees, Ph.D., $13.95
Opening a doorway to mind-altering sex, this how-to manual allows readers to expand their capacity for pleasure by learning to give and experience the amazing ecstasy of female ejaculation.

Orgasms That Will Make Her Toes Curl: The Many Amazing Ways to Climax—as Only a Woman Can
Lisa Sweet, $16.95
Beautifully sensual yet straight-talking and highly informative, this book is a modern girl's best friend when it comes to the big "oh yeah."

The Wild and Naughty Bucket List: 369 Sexy Dares to Do Before You Die

Kourtney Jason, $12.95

A provocative checklist of sexy suggestions for living an erotically adventurous life, this cool and fun list of sexual challenges dares you to break from normal routine and experience the thrill of the edge.

Wild and Sexy: The Stunning Book of Thrilling Sex Positions

Laura Leu, $14.95

The positions are hot. The techniques are erotic. And the presentation will blow readers away. *Wild and Sexy* brings it all together in a book that dramatically boosts the pleasure quotient for couples looking to spice up their sex life.

To order these books call 800-377-2542 or 510-601-8301, fax 510-601-8307, e-mail ulysses@ulyssespress.com, or write to Amorata Press, P.O. Box 3440, Berkeley, CA 94703. All retail orders are shipped free of charge. California residents must include sales tax. Allow two to three weeks for delivery.

Acknowledgments

Ben, Rita, and Bob, thank you for your unconditional love and support. The three of you make everything possible.

Stephanie Morris, your gifts of time, talent, and friendship are deeply appreciated. Thank you for helping at the perfect time.

Cameryn Moore, thank you for gracing this book with your expertise as a phone whore, a writer, and a performance artist.

Thank you also to everyone who generously contributed your real-life dirty talk examples and who allowed me to interview you and share your stories. May your bold experiences inspire many more.

And I must also express my deep gratitude to Kelly Reed, Claire Chun, and the staff at Ulysses Press for this opportunity to encourage nice girls to discover their pleasure and give it voice.

About the Author

Dr. Ruth Neustifter is a recognized relationship expert specializing in sexual communication and education as well as recovery from intimate partner violence. She works with a diverse range of individuals and relationships, conducts original research, offers workshops, and is available for professional consultation. She is also active in mentoring fellow sex-positive professionals from a range of disciplines.

University instructor, published author, respected presenter, and dedicated activist, Ruth Neustifter holds a doctoral degree in Child and Family Development with specializations in Couples and Family Therapy and Qualitative Research. She began her training, research, and work in the areas of relationships, sexuality, and recovery from intimate partner violence over a decade ago. During that time she has taught and presented in venues ranging from independent sexuality boutiques to university classrooms and international conferences. Her writing can be found throughout the Internet and in publications including the *Journal of Feminist Family Therapy* and *The Electronic Journal of Human Sexuality*.

Affectionately known by her clients and coworkers as Dr. Ruthie, she makes her home in the Washington DC area with her partner and pets. She offers private appointments and professional consultation services internationally, with appointments in person, by phone, and online.